New England Insurance Exchange

Tenth anniversary of the New England insurance exchange

January 6, 1893

New England Insurance Exchange

Tenth anniversary of the New England insurance exchange
January 6, 1893

ISBN/EAN: 9783337108892

Printed in Europe, USA, Canada, Australia, Japan

Cover: Foto ©Suzi / pixelio.de

More available books at **www.hansebooks.com**

TENTH ANNIVERSARY

OF THE

New England Insurance Exchange

HOTEL VENDOME, BOSTON, MASS.

JANUARY 6, 1893.

1893

THE STANDARD PUBLISHING COMPANY

BOSTON, MASS.

Officers, 1893.

PRESIDENT :

C. B. FOWLER.

VICE-PRESIDENTS :

E. C. BRUSH.   E. C. NORTH.

A. C. ADAMS.

EXECUTIVE COMMITTEE :

J. L. KENDIG, Chairman.

G. W. HINKLEY.   J. J. DOWNEY.

C. L. WOODSIDE.   G. HERBERT IDE.

SECRETARY :

C. M. GODDARD.

NEW ENGLAND INSURANCE EXCHANGE,

January 6, 1893.

The tenth anniversary of the New England Insurance Exchange was celebrated by a banquet at Hotel Vendome, Boston, Friday evening, Jan. 6, 1893. It was a successful and auspicious event, being attended by nearly two hundred fire underwriters, among whom were some of the most prominent officers and managers in the country.

The celebration began with a reception at 4 o'clock, P. M., in the hotel parlors. At 6 o'clock the members and their guests repaired to the dining room. The tables were arranged in four rows the length of the hall and crossed at the top by another at which were seated the principal guests of the evening, President Emerson occupying the centre. On his right were George L. Chase, president of the Hartford Fire; D. W. C. Skilton, president of the Phœnix of Hartford; J. H. Washburn, vice-president of the Home; J. Montgomery Hare, manager of the Norwich Union, and George P. Sheldon, president of the Phenix of Brooklyn. On his left were George S. Merrill, insurance commissioner of Massachusetts; John C. Paige of Boston; Samuel P. Blagden, manager of the North British; James F. Dudley, secretary of the Ætna; Osborn Howes, Jr., secretary of the Boston Board, and F. C. Moore, president of the Continental. The ends of the table were occupied by U. C. Crosby, historian, and Amos Sherman, toastmaster of the occasion.

Other guests and members of the Exchange present were as follows:

GUESTS.—Robert B. Beath, secretary National Board; C. L. Hedge, president New York State association; S. B. Stearns, president, and S. C. Eastman, secretary, New Hampshire Board of Underwriters; C. M. Goddard, secretary New England Insurance Exchange; O. P. Clark, ex-secretary New England Insurance Exchange; Charles W. Whitcomb, fire marshal, Boston; C. M. Ransom of THE STANDARD; H. R. Hayden of the *Weekly Underwriter;* Charles C. Little, secretary, J. W. Barley, general agent, and Everett U. Crosby, manager sprinkler department, Phenix of Brooklyn; T. Y. Brown of New York; J. J. Cornish, special agent Home; Thomas F. Goodrich, vice-president Niagara Fire; George Wensley, superintendent of agencies Norwich Union; Henry C. Short, secretary Fireman's Fire, Boston; Charles E. Chase, assistant secretary Hartford Fire; J. A. Macdonald, president Queen; William B. Clark, president Ætna; W. W. Underhill, president United States Fire; M. A. Stone, president, and C. D. Barton, general agent, Greenwich; A. J. Wright, president Springfield F. & M.; Benjamin J. Ackerman, manager State Investment & Insurance Company of San Francisco; C. H. Waite, general agent, and George E. Brewer, superintendent of agencies, Sun Insurance Office, Frank Jones, president, A. F. Howard, secretary, Granite State; Francis Peabody, president American of Boston; George A. Park, secretary, and Charles S. Park, assistant secretary, First National; J. C. French, secretary, and G. Byron Chandler, treasurer, New Hampshire Fire; W. T. Barton, president Merchants', Providence; F. O. Affeld, manager Hamburg Bremen; J. McCord, assistant general agent Hanover; J. L. Caven, vice-president United Fireman's; James Nichols, president National Fire; George W. Hoyt, assistant manager of the Liverpool & London & Globe; Thomas L. Churchill, chief inspector New England Bureau of United Inspection; H. E. Russell, local agent, Boston.

MEMBERS.—A. C. Adams, A. C. Anthony, G. H. Allen, Henry N. Baker, S. S. Banks, N. S. Bartow, H. S. Bean, A. L. Berry, George B. Bodwell, W. A. R. Boothby, W. H. Boutell, J. H. Burger, A. S. Burrington, M. R. Buxton, Frederick B. Carpenter, O. B. Chadwick, Arthur A. Clarke, S. B. Clarke, J. B. Cornish, E. B. Cowles, W. F. Dearborn, Jr., D. J. DeCamp, Thomas H. Dooley, J. J. Downey, J. D. Eaton, W. L. Fay, W. G. Fitch, H. V. Freeman, James M. Forbush, C. B. Fowler, G. A. Furness,

A. B. Gillette, William R. Gray, J. F. Hastings, A. T. Hatch, George W. Hinkley, II. L. Hiscock, J. Edward Hollis, Samuel G. Howe, G. Herbert Ide, Henry J. Ide, G. R. Kearley, C. W. Kellogg, George E. Kendall, J. L. Kendig, Henry A. Knabe, James II. Leighton, George E. Macomber, Charles E. Macullar, N. A. McNeil, George Neiley, E. C. North, Thomas L. OBrion, Charles D. Palmer, F. D. Parsons, S. G. Parsons, Daniel Prentice, S. B. Reed, J. J. Reid, C. II. Rice, W. F. Rice, Fred Samson, Frank W. Sargent, Albert W. Sewall, George Shaw, George L. Shepley, C. F. Simmons, A. K. Simpson, A. K. Slade, Jr., Charles M. Slocum, W. II. Smith, H. II. Soule, F. II. Stevens, C. E. Stickney, R. James Tatman, George W. Taylor, W. T. Teale, James E. Tillinghast, G. K. Tinker, Henry R. Turner, E. L. Watson, F. A. Wetherbee, II. S. Wheelock, Henry F. Whitney, B. B. Whittemore, C. H. Wilkins, II. P. Wood, Silas P. Wood, A. L. Frisby, W. B. McCray, William II. Hellyar, F. T. Noble.

HONORARY MEMBERS.—C. G. Smith, manager Factory Insurance Association of Hartford; George P. Field, manager Royal and Pennsylvania, Boston; Curtis Clark, insurance, Boston; C. E. Galacar, vice-president Phœnix, Hartford; E. G. Richards, secretary, and B. R. Stillman, assistant secretary, National, Hartford; J. C. Hilliard; F. A. Colley, superintendent of agencies, London & Lancashire; G. O. Carpenter, insurance, Boston; A. H. Wray, assistant manager Commercial Union; Samuel J. Whyte, general agent Springfield F. & M.

The following is a full stenographic report of the after-dinner exercises:

Mr. Emerson—I need not say to you, gentlemen, that the meaning and significance of this gathering is the commemoration of the tenth anniversary of the organization of the New England Insurance Exchange; but I must not forget to remind you, as we sit around this festive board, that " not only to feastful mirth is this white hour assigned, but also to sweet discourse— the banquet of the mind." It is with sincere pleasure that I extend to you all fraternal greetings, and on behalf of the Exchange, especial cordial welcome to *you*, our invited guests. We gratefully recognize that in honoring us by your presence on this occasion, you show your approval of what we have done in the past and encourage us to go forward with renewed energy and devotion to the principles of our association towards the com-

plete accomplishment of the purposes for which the Exchange
was founded. It is not my purpose at this time to refer to the
causes which led to the organization of our association, nor to
enlarge upon the work which we have done during the past ten
years in promoting the common interests of fire insurance in
New England. This duty has been assigned to our honored first
president, and I am most happy to introduce our historian, Mr.
U. C. Crosby.

ADDRESS OF U. C. CROSBY.

Mr. President and Gentlemen: The record of ten years in any
line of business is interesting and instructive. The last decade
has been marked by special and most wonderful advance, and
the profession of underwriting has not been an exception.

The fire insurance business in New England during the years
1881, 1882, and 1883 was in a demoralized condition, and outside the territory the situation was little better. Each company
acted independently of the others on nearly every question. Sus-
picion of trickery was rife. If the special agent of a company
was known to visit a local agent or a risk, other specials immediately followed to determine, if possible, the purpose of the
first. The assured put up their insurance at auction; advertised
for sealed bids for the lowest rate or premium. The cost of insurance received practically no consideration; in fact, was an
unknown quantity. There was a mad rush for business on the
part of local and special agents, and the last man on the ground
usually captured the risk. All manner of schemes to secure
business were considered and practiced, with no concert of action
on the part of the companies and with no attempt at improvement or consideration of general principles of underwriting.
With the feelings of distrust and jealousy entertained by each
company, the conditions were such as to arouse on the part of
underwriters great anxiety and gloomy forebodings, and give to
the assured a sense of insecurity and hearty contempt for our
business methods. Today every agent in New England has

joined hands with his associates in the consideration and proper conduct of the insurance business. Every risk is rated and on a fairly uniform basis. Practical questions of underwriting are considered and put into operation. Our companies act together in investigating hazards, in methods of improvement, and the inspection of risks. Now in place of distrust, pronounced demoralization, and disintegrating conditions, a general feeling of friendliness, confidence, and respect exists between our companies, agents, and the insuring public. Shall we seek for the leading factor in this change?

In December, 1882, a little company of field men met in an office on Congress street to consider special danger in a certain locality. Their success prompted the idea that such an association might be made permanent. A committee was appointed to consider the matter and, acting on their report, Jan. 6, 1883, just ten years ago today, came into existence the moving spirit in the transformation—the New England Insurance Exchange. It will be the duty of your historian to name the personnel of the Exchange, to briefly outline its principles of operation, the nature of its work, its methods and general results.

The Exchange was organized with a membership of	36	
Joined since	181	
		217
Loss by death	13	
Retired entirely from insurance business or transferred to other fields or departments	52	
Promoted to the official staff of our companies	18	
		83
Leaving our present membership............................		134

Membership is confined to persons regularly engaged in or having charge of the New England field work of any fire insurance company and is entirely personal. Its object is the systematic interchange of information and co-operation among field men.

The Exchange has taken in charge and rated, mostly by schedule, the following classes of property:

> Boot and shoe factories.
> Cotton and woolen mills.

Electric light stations.

Paper, pulp, and leather-board mills.

Summer hotels.

Risks protected by automatic sprinklers.

Each class is in charge of a committee. Risks are rated by personal examination and schedule applied in which charges are made for the defects and credit given for improvements, and each class published in a separate book. This system of rating gives uniform consideration, encourages improvements, and has proved satisfactory to all parties interested.

The number of risks rated and published in each tariff:

Boot and shoe factories	1,671
Cotton and woolen mills	778
Electric light stations	200
Paper, pulp, and leather-board mills	219
Summer hotels	561
Manufacturing risks examined and under jurisdiction of the factory improvement committee	1,159
	4,588

All property not included in the above ratings, but under the jurisdiction of the Exchange, is rated through the medium of local board organizations, except in a few cases where agents are so located that a local board could not be formed, in which case rates are made and published by the committee. Each local board is under the direct supervision of a standing committee of the Exchange, selected on the principle that each agency shall have a representative on the committee. Number of local boards under Exchange committees one hundred and nineteen (119).

The value, importance, and magnitude of the interests entrusted to our care is shown by the following table—giving the amount written, premiums collected, losses paid, percentage of loss to amount insured and to premium by stock companies in each of the New England States for the ten years covering the period of the Exchange existence—the year 1892 being an estimate, and for the purpose of comparison the three years subsequent to the organization of the Exchange being given:

	Risks Written.	Premiums Received.	Average Rate.	Losses Incurred.	Risks.	Premiums.
1880.						
Maine...	$65,920,755	$760,396	.0115	$473,459	0.71	62.29
N. H....	39,674,581	481,221	.0121	278,261	0.70	57.85
Vermont	......	238,055	....	119,270	...	50.11
Mass....	493,854,496	4,158,751	.0084	2,638,806	0.53	63.58
R. I.....	57,177,271	535,908	.0093	158,132	0.27	29.50
Conn....	130,111,556	1,242,395	.0095	516,693	0.47	42.48
Totals.	$786,738,659	$7,416,726	.0091	$4,184,621	0.53	56.42
1881.						
Maine...	$67,217,625	$774,256	.0115	$555,546	0.82	71.76
N. H....	41,296,823	501,404	.0121	376,145	0.91	75.07
Vermont	......	284,767	....	159,911	....	55.43
Mass....	516,098,999	4,450,426	.0086	2,498.207	0.48	56.14
R. I.....	61,537,859	561,130	.0091	265.658	0.43	47.34
Conn	147,257,456	1,366,074	.0093	630,556	0.42	46.36
Totals.	$833,408,762	$7,938,057	.0091	$4,486,023	0.53	56.50
1882.						
Maine...	$71,213.277	$851,681	.0119	$643,780	0.90	75.64
N. H....	42,403,451	526,738	.0124	360,823	0.85	68.59
Vermont	24,047,740	295.641	.0122	238,315	0.99	80.62
Mass....	548,641,643	4,701,185	.0086	4,271,692	0.77	90.88
R. I.....	62,697.262	579,360	.0092	376,789	0.60	65.04
Conn....	148,913,978	1,364.583	.0091	971,239	.067	71.41
Totals.	$897,917,351	$8,319,188	.0092	$6,862,638	0.76	82.49
Totals 1880—1882.						
Maine...	$204,351,657	$2.386,333	.0111	$1,672,785	0.82	70.09
N. H.....	123,374,855	1,509,363	.0122	1,015,229	0.82	67.26
Vermont.	24,047,740	818,463	.0122	517,496	0·99	63.23
Mass	1,558,595,138	13,310.362	.0086	9,408,705	0.85	70.68
R. I	181,412,392	1,676,398	.0092	800,579	0.44	47.75
Conn	426,282,990	3,973,052	.0093	2,118,488	0.49	53.57
Totals.	$2,518,064,772	$23,673,971	.0091	$15,533,282	0.60	65.61
1883.						
Maine...	$75,965,994	$957,581	.0126	$599,741	0.79	62.14
N. H....	43,850,997	554,035	.0126	349,931	0.79	63.16
Vermont	24,903.384	317,365	.0128	320,827	1.28	101.11
Mass....	555,758,070	5,249,660	.0094	3,166,754	0.57	60.43
R. I	61,554,324	627,659	.0102	366,664	0.59	58.42
Conn....	158,654,833	1,530,138	.0091	1,037,596	0.65	67.81
Totals.	$920,687,602	$9,236,474	.0100	$5,841,513	0.63	63.25
1884.						
Maine...	$72.752.045	$988,452	.0135	$749,864	1.03	75.89
N. H....	44,108,452	608,735	.0138	307,597	0.69	50.58
Vermont	25,634,193	340.735	.0132	197,401	0.77	57.93
Mass....	500,057,935	5,398,417	.0107	3,289,001	0.65	61.13
R. I.....	57,846,396	646,029	.0111	309,140	0.53	47.85
Conn....	149,880,256	1,582.534	.0105	669,832	0.44	42.30
Totals.	$850,279,277	$9,564,902	.0112	$5,522,835	0.64	57.95

1885.

Maine ...	$69,198,931	$997,832	.0147	$516,750	0.74	51.82
N. H. ...	10,836.054	132.060	.0122	46,697	0.43	35.37
Vermont.	24,077.082	343.777	.0142	156,124	0.65	45.42
Mass. ...	495.062,977	5,579,738	.0112	2,641,665	0.53	47.42
R. I.	59,219,600	680,222	.0116	229,503	0.38	33.74
Conn....	152,861,411	1,645,326	.0107	922,658	0.60	56.25
Totals.	$311,256,055	$9,378,955	.0118	$4,513,397	0.55	48.23

1886.

Maine ...	$79,056,037	$1,094,350	.0138	$1,183,391	1.49	108.56
N. H. ...	42,685,622	547.256	.0128	106,792	0.35	19.52
Vermont	26,471,112	357,889	.0135	195,512	0.73	54.64
Mass. ...	519,840,650	5,886,521	.0113	2,677,661	0.51	45.53
R. I.	63,010,528	713,314	.0113	171,926	0.27	24.10
Conn....	162,114,280	1,729,314	.0106	720,067	0.45	41.86
Totals.	$893,178,229	$10,328,644	.0115	$5,055,349	0.56	48.94

1887.

Maine...	$83,241.416	$1,143,901	.0137	$654,054	0.78	57.37
N. II. ...	54,907.446	698,699	.0127	400,011	0.72	57.30
Vermont	28,589.845	381,250	.0133	216,135	0.76	55.69
Mass....	573,023,604	6,205,626	.0108	2.657,562	0.46	42.93
R. I.	66,015,089	720,928	.0109	311,620	0.47	43.22
Conn....	167,182,877	1,742,677	.0104	858,496	0.51	59.90
Totals.	$972,960.277	$10,893,081	.0112	$5,097,878	0.52	46.79

1888.

Maine...	$80,701,943	$1,130,704	.0140	$539,092	0.66	47.70
N. H. ...	60,810,198	744,190	.0122	259,848	0.42	34.90
Vermont	39,113,015	577,486	.0147	465,461	1.19	80.60
Mass....	627,167,983	6,394,645	.0101	3,781,151	0.60	59.20
R. I.	68,827,343	759,503	.0113	759,740	1.13	100.00
Conn....	174,445,556	1,771,757	.0101	837,566	0.48	47.20
Totals.	$1,051,066,038	$11,378,285	.0108	$6,642,858	0.63	58.38

1889.

Maine ...	$89,140,620	$1,198,570	.0134	$559.411	0.62	46.60
N. II. ...	70,997,576	845,949	0.119	312,581	0.44	36.90
Vermont	42,412,460	632.347	.0149	492,063	1.16	77.80
Mass. ...	618,513,881	6,261.100	.0101	8,527.354	1.37	136.10
R. I.	70,914.144	759,873	.0106	240,762	0.33	31.60
Conn....	184,002,882	1,792,085	.0097	754,495	0.41	42.10
Totals.	$1,075,981,563	$11,489,924	.0107	$10,886,766	1.01	94.75

1890.

Maine ...	$92,836,769	$1,260,714	.0135	$726,781	0.78	57.60
N. H....	65,284,994	790,277	.0121	319,336	0.49	40.40
Vermont	32,010,421	432,486	.0135	170,247	0.53	39.40
Mass....	660,894,785	6,729,961	.0101	4,393,444	0.65	63.90
R. I.	80,194,968	797,705	.0099	429,351	0.53	53.80
Conn....	189,562,237	1,831,195	.0096	808,533	0.42	44.20
Totals.	$1,120,784,174	$11,842,338	.0105	$6,757,692	0.60	57.06

1891.

Maine...	$92,841,159	$1,248,815	.0134	$785,822	0.84	62.90
N. II....	68,560,147	818,937	.0119	307,267	0.44	37.50
Vermont	36,988,277	474,437	.0128	522,330	1.41	110.70
Mass.....	648,573,843	6,375,850	.0098	3,774,535	0.58	59.20
R. I.....	91,825,443	844,259	.0092	591,304	0.64	69.60
Conn....	195,234,620	1,839,174	.0094	705,628	0.36	38.30
Totals.	$1,133,973,489	$11,601,472	.0102	$6,686,886	0.58	57.65

1883 TO 1887 INCLUSIVE.

Maine...	$380,214,423	$5,172.116	.0136	$3,703.800	0.97	71.61
N. H....	196,388,571	2,540,785	.0129	1,211,028	0.61	47.66
Vermont	129,675,616	1,741,016	.0135	1,085,999	0.83	62.31
Mass....	2,643,743,236	28,329,962	.0107	14,432,643	0.54	50.94
R. I.....	307,645,937	3,388,188	.01101	1,388,853	0.45	40.99
Conn....	790,693,657	8,229,989	.0104	4,208,649	0.53	51.13
Totals.	$4,448,361,440	$49,402,056	.0111	$26,030,072	0.58	52.67

1888 TO 1891 INCLUSIVE.

Maine...	$355,520,491	$4,838,803	.0136	$2,611,106	0.72	53.96
N. H....	265,652,915	3,199,353	.01204	1,199,132	0.45	37.48
Vermont	150,474,173	2,116,756	.0140	1,650,101	1.09	73.23
Mass....	2,555,150,492	25,761,556	.0101	20,386,484	0.79	79.13
R. I.....	311,761,989	3,161,340	.0101	2,021,157	0.65	63.96
Conn....	743,245,295	7,234,211	.0098	3,106,222	0.41	44.94
Totals.	$4,381,805,264	$46,312,019	.0106	$30,974,202	0.70	66.40

1883 TO 1891 INCLUSIVE.

Maine...	$735,734,914	$10,010.919	.0136	$6,314,906	0.85	52.78
N. H....	462,041,486	5,740.138	.0125	2,410,160	0.53	42.57
Vermont	280,149.789	3,857.772	.0138	2,736,100	0.96	67.77
Mass....	5,198,893,728	54,091,518	.0104	34,819,127	0.66	65.04
R. I.....	619,407,835	6,449,528	.0105	3,410.010	0.56	52.47
Conn....	1,533,938,952	15,464,200	.0101	7,314,871	0.47	48.04
Totals.	$8,830,166,704	$95,714,075	.0108	$57,005,174	0.64	59.54

Estimated premium for 1892	$10,634.897
Estimated loss for 1892.................................	6,333.908
Total premium income for ten years,...................	106,348.972
Total premium loss for ten years......................	63,339,082

Under the management of the Exchange rates on certain un-profitable classes have been advanced, improvement in construc-tion and protection encouraged by reduction in rates, and the whole field re-adjusted on a basis giving our companies in ten years, in addition to new business, a net increase in premium income in our field of $16,679,000. Estimating the expense of doing business in New England at 35 per cent, a fair average, the record for three years directly preceding the organization of the Exchange shows an actual loss to our companies, and for the ten years following an underwriting profit of 5.45 per cent. We have met the deficiencies of previous years, the 1891 conflagrations in Boston and Lynn, and transferred to the profit account an amount which our conservative underwriters consider moderate and the most captious critic must admit to be the smallest margin consistent with safety and security to the policy-holder.

The practical features of its work are indicated by the organization of and care and supervision over 119 local boards, the personal examination and rating by schedule of 4,027 manufacturing establishments, and 561 summer hotels. It has been the guiding and controlling power responsible for rates which have made possible the collection of $106,000,000 in premiums, and indirectly has aided in the proper distribution of $63,000,000 to the assured. This work has been accomplished with such good judgment and discretion as to generally command the respect and confidence of our agents and the public. Differences of opinion and misunderstandings have occurred and occasional violations of the rules and rates, but they have been slight and do not appear as a factor.

We have made mistakes; we have had dark days when clouds heavily charged with elements of dissension and disintegration seemed to hang over us, threatening our very existence; yet in every case the practical good sense and sterling qualities of our members have come to the rescue. The menacing cloud has been swept away and the sky appeared brighter and clearer than before. Every year has shown an advanced position on many questions and the yearly milestone indicates a forward movement.

There is not a non-board agency in our field or a stock company doing business in violation of the rules and rates, a record unparalled in the history of like organizations, and of which we may be justly proud.

Among the underlying causes contributing to the success of the Exchange, the following should be especially noted:

First. The principle noted in our constitution.—"It is not the purpose or the desire of the New England Insurance Exchange to attempt to interfere in any way with the prerogatives of the executive officers of the companies or any organization of which they may be members." Each member of the Exchange has duties assigned and authority delegated to him by his company. In its work and operations it has been clearly the wish and intention of the Exchange to keep strictly within the limit of power and authority thus delegated to its members. To this underlying principle is largely due the hearty support given by our companies.

Second. The co-operation and confidence of our local agents. —From the first it was the governing principle and rule of the Exchange to obtain the support and assistance of our agents in the making of rates and in the general conduct of local agency business. The right to dictate to local boards and to make rates independent of them has always been admitted—we have so rated schedule and sprinkled risks—but outside of these the power has been exercised only in rare cases. The Exchange local committees have in general performed their work with good judgment and discretion, and the local agents have been made to feel that they are an important factor, and they have worked with us, not as subordinates, but as associates and co-laborers. They are our friends today and with hardly an exception are hearty supporters of local boards and of the New England Insurance Exchange.

Third. The self-reliance of our members.—The members of the Exchange have attended to their duties and have not referred perplexing questions to the home office. With a knowledge of the general policy of their companies, a proper understanding of the nature and extent of the details delegated to them, they have made a study of the ever changing and varying conditions, and within the lines laid down have assumed responsibility. The work accomplished is not the result of the special ability of a few, but of the united action of an association of field men in thorough touch with their agents, and with an intimate knowledge of the peculiarities of the business in different localities, and of the whims and prejudices of their agents and the assured. If we had wandered far into forbidden fields and encroached on the prerogatives of our companies, we should have heard from them, and with no uncertain sound. The fact that they have given us their hearty support indicates that we have produced what they desire—good results.

Fourth. The honor and good faith of our members.—This is the foundation on which the Exchange is builded; destroy it and the whole superstructure will fall. Members of the Exchange believe in the honor and integrity of their associates. If this was not true we should not be here tonight celebrating ten years of uninterrupted prosperity.

Fifth. Freedom from non-board competition.—The Exchange has acted on the underlying principle that "a chain is not stronger than its weakest link;" that we would give everyone an interest and a part in the work; the weakest a hearing, that we would act for the interest of all, but that we would not have non-board competition. Three or four attempts have been made to establish non-board agencies, but a straight-forward, manly protest and personal presentation of the situation to the parties interested resulted in removing the difficulties and closing the agencies. Had we not succeeded prompt dissolution of the Exchange would have been the result. We promised our agents that if they would unite with us in the consideration and making of rates and in the proper conduct of our business, we would give them protection. How well we have kept our promise the record will show. This principle might seem to indicate an element of weakness; it has proved a tower of strength. Without this vital and unwritten law we could not present tonight a field free from this competition.

Your historian would gladly linger to indulge in personal reminiscences. He would like to mention the work of committees and of members; would like to mention by name the secretaries of the Exchange, men of special ability and fitness for their position, and to whom we owe much of our success;

would like to give the names of members who have graduated into high official positions, members of whom we may well be proud—but time will not permit. We will only pause to pay tribute to the practical judgment characterizing the deliberations of the Exchange and the work of its committees; the honor, integrity, and manly qualities of its members, and the strict fidelity with which they, to the best of their ability, have worked and cared for the interests of their companies.

The history of the Exchange would not be complete without mention of two organizations closely allied with and virtually a part of us: the Insurance Library Association and the New England Bureau of United Inspection. The Insurance Library Association was incorporated under Massachusetts laws for educational, historical, scientific, and social purposes connected with or relating to fire and marine insurance. The membership is limited to Exchange members and representatives of companies contributing to its fund. Its success is largely due to the earnest work of a member and former president of the Exchange. It has already accumulated a large library of legal and statistical works; also maps and surveys arranged in convenient form for ready reference, and in pleasant rooms open during business hours and free to members and visitors. It is one of the best of its kind in this country and its value to underwriters will continue to increase.

The Bureau of United Inspection was brought into existence through the medium of an Exchange committee, and while it was not deemed best to make the bureau a part of the Exchange its management has always been largely in the hands of Exchange members. It has been a success from its start, in a practical way developing and working out a principle of special importance to underwriters.

The part the Exchange has taken in certain practical questions occupying the minds of underwriters at the present time is worthy of special mention: co-insurance, united action in the inspection and protection of property, schedule rating, and the relations of the underwriter to the insuring public.

CO-INSURANCE.—The principle that rates should be made on the same relative amount of insurance to value has long been considered by underwriters, but the Exchange was the first organization to put the principle into practical operation. In 1885 a committee was appointed to take the subject under consideration and the companies were asked to give their approval to its application in New England; a minority expressed disapproval and no general action was taken, but the principle was gradually applied in special ri-ks and rates by a few local boards. Interest was aroused by the discussion; our companies and organizations outside of our territory took up the question and in many localities anticipated us in its broader application. The closing month of last year was made memorable by the adoption of the co-insurance principle and its application on all specifically rated risks within " Exchange " jurisdiction, and on practically the same basis recommended in 1885.

INSPECTIONS.—The method generally adopted by our companies for the inspection of their business has been subjected to grave criticism. The frequent examination of each risk by the special agent of every company interested is expensive both to the companies and the assured. It is an inspection which does not improve the risk and is most exasperating to the owner of large property. With the increase in the number of field men, inspections increased and the members of the Exchange were quick to feel the demoralizing effect on the assured. Earnest consideration was given to the subject and resulted in the formation of the New England Bureau of United Inspection. The reform once started extended to other fields and the system will doubtless continue to be enlarged, improved, and extended to all classes of property.

SCHEDULE RATING.—The Exchange has taken special interest in this system. It was the first to apply a schedule to boot and shoe factories, hat factories, and electric light stations, and limited mercantile schedules have been used in rating certain localities. The system of rating which gives to each risk consideration on its merits, commends itself to the judgment of all.

Our experience on this point has been most pronounced and emphatic. We have had the least trouble, in fact, *no* trouble worth considering with rates based on a schedule. It has made clear the fact that it is the only basis on which we can advance rates or place them on a paying basis without a vigorous protest on the part of the assured. Schedule rating will change the business of underwriting from a game of chance to one of science.

THE RELATION OF THE UNDERWRITER TO THE INSURING PUBLIC.—Insurance companies are to a great extent public institutions. The business interests of this country are to a large measure dependent upon the security given by fire insurance. It is the duty of underwriters to study to make the burden as light as possible. The Exchange has been a pronounced factor in this work. It was the first on the part of stock underwriters to make investigation into the system of antomatic sprinkler protection. The work in this line has been especially thorough and practical and has received the confidence and support of the manufacturers.

The work of the Exchange has not been limited to the making of rates producing a profit to our companies. It has made a study of construction, of hazards, of protection; it has interested the assured in the improvement of his risk, has reduced the cost of his insurance and made him our friend; has served the true interests of the insuring public, and it is in this line that the best work has been done. We serve our companies best when we serve the public best.

The underwriting of the future will consist, not in advancing rates, but in making systematic and intelligent investigation into hazards and causes of fires that they may, as much as possible, be eliminated, and in the scientific examination into the practical application of protection. The business of underwriting will be made a profession and conducted on a scientific basis; the objective point being a low and diminishing loss ratio and cost of insurance, with a reasonable and more uniform balance of profit. There has been a tremendous advance during the last decade.

Our underwriters are not men to step backward; they cannot remain stationary—they must move forward; and in the future, when present questions of doubt and uncertainty have been solved, when theories have been exploded or become facts, it will be recorded that the original moving spirit in investigation and reform was the association whose tenth anniversary we, this day, celebrate—The New England Insurance Exchange.

Mr. Emerson—It gives me great pleasure to announce the next speaker, who I am sure needs no words of introduction to a company like this—a man whom we all know and delight to honor, whose name is a tower of strength in all that pertains to correct principles of fire insurance, and whose active participation in the business of underwriting antedates our anniversary by more than four decades, Hon. George L. Chase, president of the Hartford Insurance Company.

ADDRESS OF GEORGE L. CHASE.

Mr. President and Gentlemen: I feel that a little explanation is due to those whom I see before me as to how I happen to be here tonight. Your eloquent and silver-tongued president came to Hartford a few weeks ago, ostensibly to talk about the co-insurance clause, and came into my office. I felt that he had something on his mind that was not expressed at the beginning, and my anticipations were verified when, after talking about the co-insurance clause and discussing it fully, he said, "The New England Exchange is to have a banquet, and I want to extend an invitation to you to attend it." I said, "I am a very busy man, as you know, and it is doubtful whether I can go." But finally I consented to come down. Then he told me that I was expected to make a speech. Then I rebelled. But in an unfortunate moment I yielded, and I am here with you tonight.

His object in bringing me here I did not quite understand at that time. I understand now, from what he has said, why he brought me here. It was to show you an old underwriter, a sort of antique, and I think it is quite possible, as I look into the faces of these young men, who have heard of me but have never seen me before, that they may have the feeling that an agent of ours at London, Ontario, once had. In 1868—Mr. Coit was then our secretary—I was called to Chicago. I went through Canada by the great western railway. Wishing to see our agent at London, Mr. Dempster, I telegraphed him to meet me at the station on the arrival of the train. The train arrived there a little sooner than I expected, and I was sitting with a little silk cap on my head and was not looking like the most dignified sort of man. I stepped out on the platform to look for Mr. Dempster, but found no man looking for me. I thought perhaps the dispatch had not reached him, which proved to be the case. I walked up the platform and saw a large, brawny scotchman, who, it seemed to me, must be Mr. Dempster. Although I had corresponded with him I had never seen him, but it seemed to me that he must be a man of that type. Stepping up to him I asked, "Is this Mr. Dempster?" He said, "Yes." I said, "I am Mr. Chase, the president of the Hartford." Said he "Mr. Coit, is it?" "No," said I, "Mr. Chase, the president of the company." "No," said he, "I think this must be Mr. Coit." "No," said I, "Mr. Chase." "What," said he, "Mr. Chase, the president of the old Hartford?" I said, "Yes, sir," as meekly as I could. "Well," said he, "I thought the president of the old Hartford was an old man with white hair and white beard—one of these men that comes down to the office in his carriage at 10 o'clock in the morning."

If I had looked like my friend on the left here (the president) or my friend Mr. Hilliard, I would have answered the purpose. I never filled the bill; I never expect to. I am not so vain as to have you think that I am not an old man; although we old men after we get to be a certain age, as my friend on the left (the president) can testify, do not like to say very much about it. And yet, gentlemen, old as I am, I count it one of the pleasantest occasions of my life to be here tonight and to meet so many gentlemen. The president has told you that I have been a long time in the business. I know I have. I know I am

giving myself away when I tell you that I have been nearly fifty
years in the business—over forty-five years—but you will excuse
that. Mr. Hilliard will set me down as giving away my age,
but I cannot help it. It is a pleasant thing to be here. I came
here expecting to find few gentlemen that I knew; I find scores
of them. And what gives me greater pleasure than anything
else is to meet the younger members of the fraternity, the men
who are to fill my place and the places of the other gentlemen
here tonight. And I tell you I have never seen an assemblage
of men in my life that carried in their faces such marks of intelligence, such readiness to grasp a subject, and such evidences of
diligence and enterprise as I see in the countenances of these
men who are to take up this great business and carry it forward
—one of the greatest businesses of the country. The men of the
New England Insurance Exchange have nobly carried forward
this work.

Before I go farther I want to say how highly I appreciate the
work you have done. Ever since your organization ten years
ago, it has been our pleasure to co-operate with you, and we have
always had our old and honored representative with you, and I
believe he has done faithful service. It has been my pleasure to
be with you as often as I could come from the home office. The
outcome of the work that has been inaugurated and carried on
by you here, none of us at this time can tell. You have builded
better than you know yourselves, and I believe that the work
which you have begun will be carried forward and that a new
era is about dawning upon the business of underwriting. We
are carrying on this business more intelligently than it has ever
been conducted before; and in this field I know that you gentlemen who have this business to carry on can safely be trusted.

I have been set down on the programme for an address. It
comes home to me very keenly that "Some are born great, some
achieve greatness, and some have greatness thrust upon them."
I feel that I have tonight this distinction thrust upon me. I will
endeavor to do as well as I can, but what I shall say to you will
be of the past. The future is to be made by the gentlemen that

I see before me. My topic is "Underwriting and its Methods Forty Years Ago." In speaking on this topic I shall of necessity refer to some matters prior to 1850 and give you some personal reminiscences.

The number of stock insurance companies in existence forty years ago was comparatively small. Many of the large companies of today were not in existence. The Phœnix of Hartford, the Home and Continental of New York, and the Phenix of Brooklyn were organized in 1853, and a host of companies have been organized since that time. Some are still in existence, but many of them have retired from business. I tried to secure from the Massachusetts insurance department some data as to the number of companies doing business in Massachusetts in 1850, but have failed, for no detailed statements were required of companies of other states or of foreign companies until 1856.

In April, 1837, an act was passed requiring that insurance offices in Massachusetts incorporated with a specific capital should make reports to the secretary of the commonwealth. The first report made to the legislature is dated Jan. 22, 1838, and was submitted by John P. Bigelow, secretary of the commonwealth. There were in existence at that time and reports were made to the secretary by thirty-nine companies. These thirty-nine companies had an aggregate nominal capital of $9,415,000. Twenty-nine companies were located in Boston. Ten were located outside, at Gloucester, Lynn, Marblehead, Springfield, Fair Haven, New Bedford, Plymouth, Provincetown, and Nantucket. The capital of the Boston companies was $7,450,000, and of the ten outside companies $1,965,000. There is no evidence on record as to how much of this capital was paid up. From the best sources of information it is believed to have been but a very small portion of their nominal capital. These reports were very meagre, and gave no data as to the amount of business transacted.

This method of reporting was continued until 1856. Few of the companies reporting in 1856 are now in existence, among them are the Springfield Fire & Marine, which was organized in 1849, and the Holyoke of Salem, which was organized and commenced business in 1843, and four Boston companies.

About the year 1855 the insurance department of Massachusetts was organized, and three commissioners appointed. They made their first report in 1856. In the commissioners' report for 1857, they say :

" Within the last three years there has been a manifest improvement in the insurance business in this state, arising, first, from a greater interest being taken in the subject by the community; second, from better rates of premiums paid for insurance. The first element of this improvement has been educed by the impositions practised by insurance companies going into operation without any actual capital or basis of strength, and calculated only to furnish employment with lucrative salaries for parties having no regard for aught but their own private advantage." [This is the talk of the then insurance commissioners. Very likely your present commissioner (turning to Maj. Merrill) will give you some other plain talk by and by; he will, I know, if you need it.] " Such companies as (not to mention older ones) the Metropolitan of Boston, the People's Mutual, the Appleton Mutual, and the Massachusetts Fire & Marine of Ipswich. The disposition of the public to receive a policy written by any company, bearing the forms of law, as a valid insurance, made the success of such companies easy and sure for a time, but when losses occurred upon those policies the worthlessness of the companies issuing them then became apparent. After years of suffering from these filibusters, the commissioners are happy to notice and report a growing disposition in the community to effect insurance only in such companies as are able to show a substantial cash capital, or such as have a sound, reliable basis of action, joined with such character and conduct on the part of the managers as will ensure prompt and fair responses to all contracts to which such companies may be parties."

This seems to be good, sound doctrine. And, secondly, they say, "By the operation of this growing public sentiment, to which we have alluded, fraudulent or unsafe companies, either home or foreign, have been deprived of a large part of their business, and honest companies are freed from irresponsible and reckless competition, which has enabled them to advance their rates of premiums and otherwise to control and regulate their business."

In the report of the commissioners for 1857 I find only three foreign companies, the Liverpool & London & Globe, the Royal, and the Monarch of England, were doing business in Massachusetts.

In view of the great number of agents now doing business in Massachusetts, it is of interest to note the number of agents who, in 1856, represented in that state what are now the large agency companies of other states. For instance, the Ætna had in the state only ten agents, the Hartford only nine, the Home six, the Continental two, the Niagara one, the Phenix of Brooklyn one, and the Liverpool & London & Globe and the Royal each had one, located in Boston, and the entire number of agents representing fire companies outside of Massachusetts was only eighty-seven. I think I am not exaggerating in saying they are numbered now by thousands. At that time the Hartford Fire Insurance Company had only 106 agents in the country; its capital was only $150,000 and its premium receipts a little more than half a million of dollars.

The great agency system, through which the companies have built up their immense business, was even then in its infancy. We believe the credit for inaugurating the agency business is due to Hartford, and to the Hartford Fire Insurance Company. The following is a copy of the first commission issued by that company appointing an agent at Norwich, Conn. :

The Hartford Fire Insurance Company has appointed Jonathan G. W. Trumbull, Esquire, of Norwich their surveyor for said town and its neighborhood, who is also authorized to receive proposals for insurance against loss by fire, in behalf of said company.

WALTER MITCHELL,
Secretary.

HARTFORD, Dec. 17, 1810.

It is believed that the Hartford Fire Insurance Company made the first appointment of an agent, who was commissioned to countersign fire insurance policies, in this country in November, 1811. The appointments made were few and many agents were not restricted to any particular territory in which to do business. The agents in those days were men who were engaged in other businesses or professions. There were some notable men acting as agents. Hon. A. H. Bullock of Worcester, afterwards an illustrious governor of your commonwealth; Henry L Dawes of North Adams, for a long time an honored senator from Massachusetts; R. E. Ladd of Springfield, who has also held official position in the state; Isaac Davis of Worcester and other prominent and well-known men were representatives of insurance companies in their day.

The compensation to the agents was not as liberal and munificent as in these later days. In an instruction book issued by the Protection Insurance Company in 1835, I find the compensation to agents was 5 per cent upon the amount received to be paid to the office, and 50 cents on each policy. The first mention made of commissions in the office of the Hartford Fire Insurance Company was six years after its organization, when Hooker & Brewster of Middlebury, Vt., were authorized to retain for their services 50 cents on each policy. 7½ per cent was the maximum commission in those happy days.

The first book of instructions to agents was issued by the Ætna Insurance Company in 1819. In 1825 the Hartford Fire Insurance Company issued instructions to agents, giving directions in regard to forms of writing policies and securing adequate rates in order to yield a fair margin of profit, and naming rates at which business might be taken on: buildings of brick or stone, covered with tile, slate, or metal, doors and windows covered with iron, and goods not hazardous therein, 22 cents; same as above, without iron windows and doors, 25 cents; without the above requirements, 30 cents; frame buildings filled in with brick, 50 cents; buildings entirely of wood, 75 cents to $1. In 1819 the tariff on cotton mills, without picker in the mill, was 3½ per cent; with picker in the mill, 4 per cent. Of course this embraced the privilege of running their picker at night. The rate for flax mills was 3½ per cent; distilleries, 2¼ per cent. They probably sought to cheapen the price of a commodity which was so much used in those days, which accounts for the low tariff. In 1837 is the first mention of schedule rating. A standard for cotton or woolen mills was published at that time, and it seems that the Providence standard was the outcome of this schedule of 1837. In 1839 the Hartford Fire Insurance Company issued an instruction book more elaborate than anything before used.

Boldness in regard to lines in those days was notable. The first risk the Hartford Fire Insurance Company wrote was $4,000 on a builder's risk, at 12½ per cent for three months; the fifth risk was $11,000 on a gin distillery, at 1¼ per cent—again in the interest of the " good old times." They insured a cotton mill at 75 cents; the owner's dwelling house, which stood remote from the mill, was rated at 1 per cent. There is found on the records of the first year's business $20,000 on a tobacco warehouse on the James River, Virginia, at 50 cents per annum. They learned wisdom, however, by experience, and after the lapse of a few years reduced their lines.

The first record of one company's re-insuring another is of the Hartford Fire Insurance Company's re-insuring the New Haven Fire Insurance Company in 1822. The Hartford gave a bond for $150,000, being the amount of its capital, for the faithful performance of the contract. In those days, you see, they had not so much confidence in each other as they have now. The terms upon which the re-insurance was effected are not recorded, and if they were the parties would blush, no doubt, to have the low rates known. You will pardon me for referring so many times to the Hartford, but I happen to have these facts at hand, and they are interesting as showing the methods of transacting our business in those days.

The speaker received his first appointment as local agent, in August, 1847, to represent the Farmers' Mutual Fire Insurance Company of Georgetown, Mass., and will incidentally remark that before he was 21 years old he was made a director in that company. At the annual meetings, in the month of May, the directors used to go to Haverhill, to Brown's Hotel, and have a shad dinner. I am sure my friend Mr. Hilliard will remember Brown's Hotel, and Brown and his boys.

Mr. Hilliard—I have been there a great many times.

Mr. Chase—They served a good dinner and always had something with it. [Laughter.] Mr. Hilliard will testify to that fact, I know.

·Mr. Hilliard—Correct.

Mr. Chase—That face of his still speaks. Well, it was a notable occasion. I have now in my desk the second policy written at my agency, dated Aug. 12, 1847. In a few months there was added to my list of companies the New England Fire & Marine Insurance Company of Concord, N. H., and the Equitable Insurance Company of the same place. I think my friend Mr. Eastman will remember that a few years ago, being in Concord, I started out to find the old office where I used to go about once in two months to report. Looking up and down the street I saw a building which I thought was the place. I knew my friend Eastman had an office upstairs, and I went up and said, "Mr. Eastman, about where is the place where the old office of the New England Fire & Marine Insurance Company stood?" "Well," said he, "this is the very building, and this is the very room, and there is the old president's desk still standing." I presume there is where Mr. Eastman received the inspiration which has made him so successful in managing the insurance business so many years and now as an officer of the Capital Fire of Concord.

' The Holyoke and Bowditch insurance companies of Salem were added to my list afterwards. The Holyoke, I believe, is still in existence and doing business. [Laughter.] Am I right, Mr. Commissioner?

Mr. Merrill—You are.

Mr. Chase—The Holyoke is still in existence.

Mr. Merrill—Very much.

Mr. Chase—I afterwards had the agency for the People's of

Taunton, and then the People's of Worcester, which will be remembered by many of those present. This last company was organized in 1851. Mr. Sanford J. Hall, the honored and accomplished secretary of the Springfield Fire & Marine Insurance Company, was then the book-keeper in the office of the People's, and has been continuously in the business ever since, and is one of the oldest and most respected insurance officers in the country. Only the Holyoke of the companies represented in my agency is now in existence.

The first compensation which the speaker received was the policy fee, paid by the assured, ranging all the way from a dollar to a dollar and a half. Afterwards he received a commission of 5 per cent. The territory of the agency was a large one, embracing Central and Western Massachusetts and the state of Connecticut, and he ventured to write policies within a radius of ten miles of the home of the great agency companies of Hartford. Risks which the speaker could not carry in companies represented in his agency he sent to Boston to Mr. Oliver Brewster, a broker, who may be remembered by some of the gentlemen present. His office was on the northeast corner of Washington and State streets. Losses were usually adjusted by some one sent from the home office of the companies. As all the companies of my agency were mutual companies, one of the duties was to collect the assessments made from time to time to meet losses, on which I received a commission of 5 per cent.

But times have changed. The business has grown to immense proportions. The expenses for doing the business have largely increased. The agents and loss claimants have become the beneficiaries of the funds gathered by the companies, who struggle to make a little money to pay a small dividend to their stockholders. In those good old days, banquets were unheard of, and an entertainment like the one we are enjoying at this moment would have produced such a consternation as the underwriters would never have recovered from, but, as I have said, the local agents are the Crœsuses of the business at the present time, and the general and special agents are important factors in the business, and are abundantly able to indulge in luxurious entertainments of this kind, while the officers of the companies are left to struggle to make buckle and strap meet at the end of the year. But the good old times are gone. The new times have come, and we are called upon, as underwriters, to meet the exigencies that are thrust upon us, whether it be a Chicago or a Boston conflagration, and it should be a matter of pride to us all to be connected with a business that lies at the foundation of all the commercial and many of the financial transactions of the day. Let us not forget the duties we owe to our stockholders and the public, and so discharge them that they will say to us, " Well done good and faithful servants."

Mr. Emerson—I am somewhat at a loss, gentlemen, to know just how to introduce the next speaker—whether it shall be as the gifted member of the Boston School Board, or the president of the Boston Board of Fire Underwriters, or by some other one of the many titles which the gentleman so worthily bears. But after we have listened to the good things he has prepared for us tonight, you will all agree with me that the proper form should be " Our sweet singer, the poet laureate of the Exchange," Mr. B. B. Whittemore.

POEM OF MR. WHITTEMORE.

Mr. President and Gentlemen of the Exchange: I am highly honored in the introduction. To be able to do anything in aid of the educational interests of the Athens of America is indeed an honor. It is an honor to stand here as representing the Boston Board of Underwriters, a body of gentlemen in whom you have the most unbounded confidence, and whose normal condition you are accustomed to consider as seizing upon the very foremost ideas and putting them in force, and indeed, if they hesitate for consideration you lift your hands in amazement. Your president has assumed on the strength of a trifle which came under his eye to present me before you in the form in which I beg you to listen to me, and if you are disappointed you must charge the whole to his presumption.

Since Homer wrote and Virgil sung
And Milton's harp was nobly strung—
Since Dante swept his strains along
And Goethe breathed his tender song—
Since Shakepeare's pen in many a line
Revealed her spirit all divine—
The Muse has lingered here and there
To make some soul her special care,
And, heedless of its name or place,
To crown it with poetic grace.
She tarried on old England's shores
And scattered there her jewelled stores,
And smiled to see a nation won
By Browning and by Tennyson.
She soared across the ocean's deep
And touched, here, in her magic sweep,
Those wond'rous springs, that raised through her
Our Longfellow and Whittier;
'T is true her noblest gifts are brought
Where loftiest themes engage the thought,
Where sacred songs enwrap the soul,
Or patriotic numbers roll;
Where nature all her art retains,
Or passion lingers in her strains.
And yet, she guides with ardent pride
The pen that paints life's sunny side,
And turns her face with smiles o'erlit
To greet the thought that teems with wit.
Her restless spirit falters not.
Invoked in palace or in cot,
And well she heeds the cheerful call'
That bids her to the banquet hall.
Since thus her kindly forms and grace
Are fitted to this time and place,
An humble bard may seek her aid
To light the duty on him laid,
And picture in some metric range
The story of our own Exchange.

How oft we think of good old times,
Whose fame comes down in prose or ryhmes
And makes us sigh for by-gone ways
That marked the business of those days.
How it does tax our best endurance

To think of old-time fire insurance!
When, with no extras to allure them,
Men sought an agent to insure them,
Pleased, if permitted but to stand
Within his office, hat in hand,
While he from off his lofty perch
Might give their case a careful search,
Applying close discrimination,
E'en on a dwelling application—
Think, how on this with nice conditions,
Concerning fires, lights, and partitions,
The suppliant's name must be implanted
Before a policy was granted!
Oh, those were times to please the fates,
When companies decreed the rates
And agents all were quite content
With net commissions, ten per cent!
'T was then the fashion, with much sense,
The contract's language to condense;
Avoiding terms that might mislead
The humblest holder, who could read.
The genius, then, was not evolved,
Who later on the problem solved
How, with much verbage, well applied,
The public might be mystified
And led with confidence to think
That contract best, which used most ink.
Then, no one knew and few men cared
How assets stood, if fully aired,
And no one dreamed official eyes
Would be employed as public prys;
And since none else was bound to tell,
All things went merrily and well.

Thus, freed from many a modern clog,
The times moved on with steady jog,
And companies, both weak and strong
Were borne complacently along,
Content with luck, as luck might run,
Until October, Seventy-One,
When suddenly there came a shock
That caused the insurance world to rock,
And companies by scores were lost
In dread Chicago's holocaust;

Survivors gasped, dismayed, dumbfounded,
While gazing on the killed and wounded,
And, too much crippled for contention,
They forthwith talked of a convention,
To which they came—a limping lot—
With Hamlets's doubt, "To be or not."
Adorned with bandages and patches,
To cover cuts and woeful scratches;
And, after some deliberation,
They straightened up a combination.
No time was wasted in debates,
But forthwith up they put the rates,
In which procedure, though hard pressed,
The public wisely acquiesced.
Soon did the tide financial swell
With life and strength that promised well,
And confidence was all aglow,
When Boston dealt a fearful blow.
Alas, for companies again,
When scores were crippled or were slain!
And well they might be sore perplexed
To know what course they should take next.
The old time custom was with pills
To treat all sorts and kinds of ills,
And, since remedial aids were few,
That companies at that time knew,
They took the quickest from their list
And gave the rates another twist.
The patient public forthwith scowled;
Anon, they grinned and then they howled,
And, as the red-hot rates advanced,
They kicked, and swore, and madly danced,
And bade the companies beware!
There was a strain they would not bear;

E'er long they saw 'twas very true
That companies were weak and few,
And that all hands must bear the strain,
That served to build them up again.
Soon business moved with lusty tread
And companies were richly fed,
And gaily sailed upon the flood,
That bore them its life giving blood.
Their garnered wisdom was then stored

In care of a "grand central board,"
Which, in a firm administration,
Directed all that combination,
And, since the late scenes of distress
Were changed to pictures of success,
The means employed were highly lauded;
The board, itself, was well applauded.
The Greeks of old a saying had
" Whom Gods destroy they first make mad."
And some god, of this insane stamp,
Contrived to gain the insurance camp,
And make our board officials think
'Twas time to take another kink.
And so they talked in long debates
Of once more jacking up the rates.

From every side the protest came,
"For heaven's sake, do not spoil our game!
Don't touch the rates! Don't kill, we beg,
The goose that lays our golden egg.
The public ire is brimful loaded,
And with slight cause can be exploded.
For failure nothing can atone,
So, pray, let well enough alone!"
But those officials felt their trust
And, with their thumbs in armholes thrust,
And with some Vanderbiltian pride—
But not his language—they replied,
" We've got the public—none can doubt it—
What will the public do about it ?"
And, since no power could then resist,
They gave the rates another twist.
What happened? Well, there came a crash —
A rumbling and a sudden flash;
And those officials were amazed,
As wildly open-mouthed they gazed,
And saw their " soft snap," as it soared
Amid the fragment of that board.

The scene of trouble that ensued,
Was such as ne'er before was brewed.
Down went the lofty scale of rates;
In came commissions and rebates,

And every risk was fought for then
By new recruits of middlemen.
The companies in sharps or flats,
Soon quarreled like Kilkenny cats;
And all the business with a thud
Went down in vile, competing mud.
And so time went with more or less
Of tardy gains, or sore distress;
Until in Eighteen Eighty-Three
New England specials came to see
That all this internecine strife
Was wearing out the springs of life,
And that 'twas folly not to bend
Their efforts to some better end.
So, someone raised a flag of truce,
Discolored from long want of use;
Suggesting, that calm consultation
Might much improve the situation.
On that, all got them from the mire,
And, brushing up their soiled attire,
With lightened hearts and smiling faces
They left their barricaded places;
And, like good, sober men of sense,
They met in friendly confidence,
And on a bright auspicious morn
Our good Exchange was fairly born.

'Twas pleasant thus to come together —
A change from cold to balmy weather—
And now the question first in hand
Was, who should lead this lusty band?
One man there was of modest mien,
Who much of stormy times had seen
But, who through trials of the past
Had held his courage to the last,
Whose ripe convictions, though intense,
Were *sprinkled* with good, common sense.
On him all eyes at once were cast —
He was the choice from first to last,
And so by common, joint consent
He was installed first President.
This done, the assembly, one and all,
Were anxious for the opening ball—
And down they sat, good souls and true,

To look the situation through
And to devise, like careful men,
How best to act, and where and when.

All in a cluster, there they sat—
A plucky lot, no doubt of that—
Yet, all at once, by some odd freak,
All hands seemed strangely loth to speak,
A queer sensation on them hung
And placed a seal on every tongue.
What 'twas that held them none could tell,
Yet all were conscious of the spell.
Anon, there rose a dismal gloom
And sulphurous odors filled the room.
Then, suddenly, quite near a post,
Flashed out a grim and ghastly ghost,
Holding between its grinning teeth
This bold inscription in a wreath—
" *I am your Old Board in this fix,*
Departed hence in Seventy-Six—
Died, as have others of the dead,
Of gross enlargement of the head"—
Then, with a whisk it turned about
And in a blue flame faded out.
'Tis said our friends met then and there
A mighty shock—a fearful scare—
That some essayed to sing a psalm—
Some whistled, while appearing calm,
But, sing or whistle, as they might,
They trembled, sadly in their fright.

The chairman struggled to his feet,
As though he would the spectre meet,
Then cried, as it withdrew from sight,
" *Good bye, old friend, It served you right.*"
Then, turning with a ruddier glow,
Said, " Gentlemen, 'twas apropos—
We'll take this spectral hint to heart
And heed the lesson as we start.
Don't let us e'er again forget
The limitations round us set,
Nor think by our united prattle
To beat the public in a battle.
But, rather, let us clearly show

That old-time, lawless, ways ' *must go.*'
That, working to a better end,
We both have some rough ways to mend.
That, when their risks are well improved,
All dangerous elements removed,
When on the whole, and everywhere,
They fix the seal of constant care,
And, when to this they super-add
Our latest automatic fad,
We'll recognize their new estate
And meet them with a tempting rate—
Then shall we enter on a field,
That may a generous profit yield,
And, if we move with proper pace,
We'll give our Mutual friends a race."

" With that " so writes our first recorder—
" The chair declared remarks in order."
Then some one said—" that's very well,
But how shall we proceed, pray tell?
This public, we desire to handle,
Is not a colt, that we can dandle,
A gay old horse 'tis, as we'll find it
With teeth in front and heels behind it,
That long has roamed about at will
And on low rates has had its fill,
And much I doubt if all your glitter
Will serve to captivate the critter.
But, say he's caught, and we would try
Our new made harness—Watch his eye!
He's seen that sort of thing before,
When he was tired, and weak, and sore—
And, if he now but feels a strap,
'Tis ten to one he'll wince and snap
And, if a further touch he feels,
There'll sure be music at his heels.
And, if he give an old time toss,
Our plans may prove a total loss—
But now I'll tell you what we'll do,
Our agents all shall help us through.
They've known the old horse, long and well,
And all its various kinks can tell,
And with their kind, judicious care,
They'll lead and work him anywhere."

With this advice, which all thought *pat*,
The speaker ceased, and down he sat.
Then followed speeches, half a score,
Endorsing what was said before,
And out of these by evolution
Came forth our present constitution.
And to this rock for ten years past
Our policy's been anchored fast.
The public sense our plan commends,
Our agents are its hearty friends,
And with fair profits all confess
Our good Exchange a grand success.

Fain would the writer now recall
The meed of praise that's due to all,
Who served so long and still remain
The heroes of our long campaign.
But time would fail the points to tell
That mark our unique *personnel.*
We have our men of solid sense,
Our samples of fine eloquence,
Our gladiators in debate,
Our modest members—more sedate—
Our mentors, who in tangled fight
Are sure to set the business right.
Our men of courage from whose grip
' T is hard for any rogue to slip,
Our busy heads of all committees,
Who watch the factories, towns, and cities,
Our young recruits with fiery zeal
Who furnish steam to run the wheel,
Our veteran corps—smile for their sakes—
Who cheer the boys, but hold the brakes.
And now, dear friends, our first decade
Has firmly a foundation laid,
On which, with rare experience filled,
We may, henceforth, securely build.
With courage we'll pursue our way,
Since wise officials—long our stay—
Believe our purposes are right
And are our honored guests tonight.
And, since through ten years we've been tried,
We may be pardoned, conscious pride,
While urging friends both South and West

Like us, to bear each trying test,
Remembering—in our prayers—the while,
Our brothers of Manhattan Isle.

But this good measure of success
Has come, as we must now confess,
From that sublime and lasting grip,
That lies in sterling fellowship.
We've had our little sideway slips,
Our ripples from incautious lips;
But, at our work we've calmly stood
An ever trusting brotherhood.
Trusting, ah yes, e'en o'er that tide
That bore our comrades from our side.
Trusting, with faith's supremest test,
A guiding hand, a home of rest.
Then, comrades, let us forward press,
With newer faith in manliness,
With confidence in solid worth
As strongest of the powers of earth,
With faith that highest good we find
In all that benefits mankind,
With pride that still before the world
Our chosen banner is unfurled,
And, with our duties well in range,
We'll still support our good Exchange.

Mr. Emerson—I have the pleasure, now, gentlemen, of presenting to you our comrade, Col. Sherman, as our toast-master for the rest of the evening.

Mr. Sherman—*Mr. President and Gentlemen:* Pope in his " Essay on Man " said :

" Man like the generous vine supported lives,
The strength he gains is from the embrace he gives.
In their own orbits as the planets run,
And make at once their circuit round the sun,
So two consistent motions act the soul,
And one is for itself and one the whole;
Thus God and nature linked our general frame,
And bade self love and social be the same."

Our self love, as to our physical desire, has, we think, been fully satisfied in the bountiful banquet of which we have partaken ; and now the social and intellectual element in our nature craves the entertainment and the instruction which so many of the guests present are abundantly able to give. We have listened with much interest to the record of our association, so ably chronicled by our historian, and so sweetly sung by our poet; we have been greatly edified by the exceedingly interesting presentation, by a veteran in the service, of the reminiscent incidents of our profession and his showing of its progressive development during the last forty years, and it has been arranged that there shall now be introduced to you in succession several of the managers of our companies and a few of their friends who have honored this occasion and us by their presence tonight. Shakespeare uttered an important truism when he asserted that "Brevity is the soul of wit," and we trust we shall be pardoned for suggesting in this connection that it is our earnest desire and expectation that all responses to the various sentiments proposed tonight, shall be seasoned with this one element of wit.

"The Massachusetts Insurance Department," honest, conservative, and courageous in its supervision, it has proven itself second to none in its protection of legitimate underwriting and the general public. We are happy to introduce to respond to this sentiment, a gentleman, whom as the head of this department, we all esteem as "the right man in the right place," Hon. George S. Merrill.

REMARKS OF GEORGE S. MERRILL.

Mr. President, Mr. Toastmaster: I thank you, gentlemen, from my heart for the cordiality of your reception. It is pleasant to come from official duties to meet in a social and informal way the men with whom the insurance department comes in contact largely only officially, and the men for whom in my brief course of official action I have come, for their ability, their integrity, and their far-sightedness, to possess a profound respect. I confess it is a little unkind to introduce anyone after the poetry of the occasion. I have seen it stated in the newspapers that in Great Britain they are a little in doubt whom they shall choose as the poet laureate of that great nation. It seems to me they have only to come to the Boston Board of Underwriters, and if all Great Britain cannot furnish a man who can fill the bill, you have him right here at your table tonight.

I am delighted to listen to these reminiscenes of the olden time. It is pleasant for us "young fellows" to hear what these elderly men tell us of the days that have gone by. And I was glad to be informed that the local agent was the Crœsus of the fire insurance business. I never before have been thrown in contact with two hundred Crœsuses. Gentlemen, I am very glad to see you, and when you come to make your wills you can kindly remember that there is a head of the insurance department of Massachusetts upon whom you can bestow your untold millions.

I understand that this association of yours is really the first association of just this particular character in our land. Well, and I say it for the benefit of these poor, benighted sons of Manhattan Isle and other foreign countries, that Massachusetts has been quite in the habit of doing the first thing. Nearly a century and a quarter ago, in that great conflict which threw off a foreign yoke and made us a great nation, it was Massachusetts that "fired the shot heard round the world." Nearly a century later, in the conflict against rebellion and against the disintegration of our nation, it was her glad privilege to give the first martyr's blood upon the alter of her country. Massachusetts formed the first insurance department of any commonwealth in this country. Massachusetts gave to you the first standard policy of fire insurance in the land by legal enactment. Massachusetts gave you the first law for the thorough and complete investigation of the causes of the fires that occur within her borders. And if his excellency, the governor, who so kindly consented in the midst of his early duties of the year to be present for a short time, had not been compelled to go away, I would say that Massachusetts is the first Republican state to elect three times in succession a Democratic governor.

I was looking a few days ago over one of the earliest reports of the Massachusetts insurance department and I found that in 1856 we had nine fire insurance companies from other states transacting business in this commonwealth and two branches of foreign companies. Today we have eighty-five companies from other states and thirty-five branches of foreign insurance companies, which simply illustrates the growth of this business in which you gentlemen are engaged — a business which today, in my judgment, is second in importance to no other single commercial interest in this broad land of ours. The companies transacting business in Massachusetts have today $270,000,000 of assets and they have in force upon their fire insurance policies $17,000,000,000 at risk. Now, stop for a moment and consider what that means. Wipe out tomorrow, if you could, every national bank, every savings bank in the United States, and within a day the recuperative power of this country would rebuild those savings banks and those national banks, and restore confidence to business. But wipe out the fire insurance business and all the commercial interests of this country would be paralyzed and destroyed in an hour. To every man who had a dollar's worth of property every day in his life would be a day of fear and every night would be a night of terror lest his little property be wiped out and his wife and children left with nothing to sustain them.

But, gentlemen, there is one question which I think I may suggest to you. It is for your consideration; you understand it and appreciate it, but the great public with whom you deal, I fear, do not. During the year which has just closed and the year which preceded it there was wiped out by the flames in this country nearly, if not quite, $140,000,000 worth of property. It is true that the institutions you represent come in and replace to the individual that which he has lost. But the insurance companies create nothing. They simply act as the medium of collecting from the policyholders the premiums and transmitting the money to those who have lost. One hundred and forty million dollars of the commercial industry and earning power of this country in each of the two past years have gone up in smoke and gone down in ashes. While your corporations have restored from what they have collected from the people the loss which the owners have sustained, yet the creative industry of this country has suffered to the extent of $140,000,000 in each of those two years. We cannot go on in that way forever. I do not expect you are going to be quite such philanthropists as to desire that there shall be no fires in this country, because then Othello's occupation would be gone. But it is for you to impress upon the people of the country these facts, and to insist upon it that the criminal carelessness in the matter of fires that now exists throughout the length and breadth of our nation shall be stopped and that if necessary the strong arm of the law shall interpose to prevent this awful waste which is now going on, beyond conception, beyond the experience of any other country. In Massachusetts last year there was 2,874 fires. With the exception of about six hundred reported as incendiary—of which at least one-half were probably not incendiary—there are, as you look over the list as collated by the Massachusetts insurance department, less than one hundred of those fires but which were from causes which were clearly and absolutely preventable, either by better building methods or by better caution in the care of property.

Now I say it belongs to you, gentlemen, to see that some of these methods are improved and brought into more general use in the future I confess it is an embarrassment always for one who knows very little about a subject to talk to a company of experts, and the fire insurance methods in this country, today, are so complete and so well carried out that an insurance commissioner needs to know very little about fire insurance, whatsoever. I am reminded, as I speak to you, of the inquiry of the boy who asked his father, " Father, if a boy is born on the ocean, what nationality is he? " " Why, the same nationality as his father and mother, of course." " Yes," said the boy, " but supposing his father and mother are not with him and he is travelling with his aunt, then what ? "

I heed the admonition of the toast-master ; I do not propose to make you a speech. I only wish to say this: I have been impressed, during the years in which I have occupied the position of insurance commissioner of Massachusetts, with the vastly improved methods in the conduct of your business over those which, as some of these elderly gentlemen tell us "young men," have prevailed in the past. And I believe, today, that the fire insurance companies of America pay ten losses about which there is a very reasonable question where they contest one which they ought not to contest. I am sure, gentlemen, that in this association, and in all associations of this character, when you come together as you do from time to time, and look each other in the face, and clasp each other by the hand, and feel that throb of the heart which always comes as one manly man's hand clasps another's, you will improve your own social condition and you will benefit yourselves. I wish the New England Insurance Exchange the most abundant and unbounded prosperity in all the years of the future.

Mr. Sherman—" Underwriting Organizations."

" Whoever thinks a perfect piece to see,
Thinks what ne'er was, nor is, nor e'er shall be."

Perfection is not a characteristic of human institutions. In their primitive existence crudeness and uncertainty are stamped upon all the enterprises of man. Only by a progressive development through successive stages of experience is the state of highest excellence or approximate perfection attained. Insurance methods and organizations as well as science and society are subject to evolution. We will introduce to respond to this sentiment a gentleman whose long and successful experience in underwriting will enable him to speak wisely on this subject, Mr. D. W. C. Skilton, president of the National Board of Fire Underwriters.

REMARKS OF D. W. C. SKILTON.

Gentlemen: Mr. Chase rarely puts his foot in it. He did tonight, and I feel it my duty to rebuke him a little. All Englishmen speak of going up to London. Mr. Chase said

he had come down to Boston. The rest of us have come up.
While listening to his remarks and looking the venerable gentleman over, it occurred to me that it should be a source of
gratification to all the rest of us that we really don't belong to
that clan of gum-eyed veterans that he is connected with.
[Pantomine of handshaking between the speaker and Mr.
Chase.]

Mr. Toastmaster, I feel it an honor to be called out at this
early moment in the list of toasts, for while you are dazed with
the glorious and beautiful things that you have already heard
you will not be badly strained in listening to what I shall say.
The few remarks that I make I imagine will be something like
a tinkling cymbal compared with the symphony of jewels that
you soon will have. I suppose it is a fact that most gentlemen
have ambition—some one great single ambition during their
life. Speaking of a friend who is gone before, the late President Goodnow of the Ætna, we are told that once on a time
when he was connected with a manufacturing establishment in
the state of Massachusetts, this little state we are now in, looking
at an Ætna policy he remarked that his ambition would be satisfied and filled if he could ever become secretary of that company. His ambition was more than fulfilled ; he became the head
of that great, old institution. For myself I don't know that I
ever had an ambition, unless it was one during my boyhood
days. A new railroad had been built through our town, and we
saw the first gallant sons of Erin who ever visited that little
village. We were afraid of them, and almost everyone bought a
dog and the men with families stayed at home most of the time
for a few weeks. Well, very soon the trains began to run, and I
discovered that the principal man on the passenger train was the
fellow that turned the brake on the baggage car and handled the
trunks. Then my father talked with me about my plans for the
future and asked me what I had in view. I told him that if I
could become the brakeman on that passenger train and on the
baggage car I should be satisfied. He said there was a buck-
saw out in the wood yard, and he would like to see it in the

works right off. I certainly never had the ambition to make a speech here in Boston near these tea-washed shores, on this classic ground where fair Harvard's sons have been digging for roots since the early morning of this new world. But here I am; the results you must accept.

Mr. President, I promised you a few weeks since that if I was able to come over to this beautiful city I would make a few remarks regarding underwriting organizations. It is my intention to make just as few as possible, keeping my promise to the letter. And still this paper does look formidable. Right here, gentlemen, I ask you kindly that if I make mention of that fearful institution called the National Board you will not be weary—that is, in the outset; you will be weary before I get through, I concede that, but don't get weary when you hear the word mentioned. Now for my text and sermon.

I assert in the outset that the principle of fraternal association and co-operation is as old as society and government, and as beneficent, when wisely applied, kept free from greed and power, and is not arbitrarily exercised for selfish ends. The association of underwriters together in national and department organizations has, in my opinion, elevated the standard of the business, broadened and liberalized insurance contracts, and the business has been greatly benefited by the interchange of thought and ideas, and the members aided largely in developing the interests entrusted to their care. On the other hand, the insuring public have as a result received greater protection under the insurance policy, and have been taught that improvements in risks suggested by these organizations means a reduction in the price of protection. The gain has been equitably divided between the insured and the insurer. Possibly you think I might as well drop the subject right here, for I think that last phrase covers the whole subject. But it does not give me a fair chance to say a few things that I think sound pretty well, so I will go on.

So far as I know, the first board of underwriters was in existence at the time of the building of Noah's Ark. You are told that when the board of insurance survey made its report to Noah, he looked over the dimensions of that grand old craft and then raising his eyes, said, "It is a goodly ship, I am well assured." We must accept this as evidence that the ship was insured, and that the policy covered the boat as a marine, fire, and accident risk.

Kindly allow me to suggest parenthetically that the ark was one of that class of risks exceedingly popular with our good friend here, Mr. Crosby, a sprinkled risk with two sources of supply—sprinkled without and within—and we are told that the external sprinkling appliances were in full operation for forty days and forty nights. The interior was divided into three stories, and I think there is plenty of evidence that there was running water on every floor and standpipes at every point, for we are told that the ark was filled from end to end with "two of a kind."

I suppose the history of the world, if closely written, would say that other boards were organized from time to time all along down through the ages. There were some boards during the past generation throughout the United States, notably the one at New York City, and I have no doubt it will surprise many here to learn that the organization of the National Board of Underwriters was suggested at a meeting of the New York local board in April, 1866. That meeting appointed a committee of three gentlemen, Messrs. E. W. Crowell, D. A. Heald, and George W. Hope, to take into consideration the calling of a convention of underwriters to consider the great questions of the hour connected with the business. Those gentlemen, as a committee, did notify the underwriters of the country generally to meet in New York, and a convention was held in July, 1866, fifty-four companies being represented.

The loyal support given to the association by the members enabled it to do most satisfactory work, and that very rapidly, too, for we find as a result of the organization of local boards and establishing of tariffs of rates generally throughout the country, that the average rate of premium that had been 68.48

for the five years 1860 to 1865, and was 82.13 in 1866, was advanced to 88½ in 1870, and was as high as 88 in 1871, the year that the first organization of the National Board practically passed into an advanced condition of decay.

The Chicago fire, of course, brought about a reaction, and in April, 1872, the board came together and a reorganization was made with a very large membership, and the result of the work done by that organization is evidenced in the average rate of premium received during the following years. In 1872 it was 92. and in 1873 it reached the very high figure of 101½, the highest figure known in the history of the business since 1860. We have no record prior to that time. These figures are based upon the reports of the companies that were doing business in the state of New York. There were a larger number of companies doing business in that state and making reports than in any other state in the Union, I think.

During the five years following 1873 the average rate steadily sagged until in 1878 it was as low as 76¾. The highest point reached since that time was in 1886, when the figure was 90.42. In 1891 it was 80.94. We have yet to learn what it was in the year 1892, but probably several points higher than during the previous year. A writer has said within a few days that the National Board of Underwriters was one of the greatest humbugs of the time. Now that depends upon how you look at it. It must be either from the standpoint of facts or figures; facts as they are and were, or figures of speech as they may be made.

The one great indisputable fact is that the National Board made possible all that has followed it in the way of reform and improvement in our business. The organization was the salvation of the fire insurance companies of this country. It was an educator both to the companies, the agents and the people. Its fall from power was because it struck upon the same rock that has wrecked so many organizations, viz: the arbitrary use of power. No underwriting organization (and we will say nothing about others) can continue a successful career if it exercises its power in a way that appears arbitrary or oppressive. The reaction is serious and the result disastrous.

The National Board at a special meeting held in 1876, when there was a disturbed feeling existing among the members, and the members were not altogether loyal to the organization, listened to a very important report made by a committee of fifteen that had been appointed during the previous April, one of the ablest committees ever created. I am sure; I was a member of it, and I happened to be on the wrong side of the question. In that report it was suggested that the organization foster state boards and secure if possible the co-operation of local boards in the making of rates. The board declined to accept the suggestion, and that was the rock on which the craft was disabled. From that time until this it has not been an organization governing the matter of rates or commissions, but the seed planted was bound to bring forth fruit, and the first crop was state boards; at first endeavoring to do their work without the co-operation of the local boards and agents; later aiming to secure that co-operation; but the effort came too late to make the move a success.

Then the department organizations, notably that of the New England Exchange, our host tonight. The lessons learned by the companies under the National Board, and the experience of the companies and the field men in the state board organizations, had taught all that it was possible that organizations might be formed that could do the work in the field better than any theretofore in existence. The work done by the New England Exchange has been so well done that the organization is practically a model one. It has been a wonderful school for field men, and the officers of the companies have learned their lessons, and today I think it is proper for me to say that if a gentleman expects to travel in the New England states as a special agent or adjuster for a fire insurance company, he can have no standing in the business unless he carries the credentials of the New England Exchange.

Now, gentlemen, let me say in all candor, we must use our power justly, but conservatively. Let us avoid the rock I have referred to and keep well in mind the fact that today the threatening danger is adverse legislation; and in all the efforts for any great radical reform we should aim to educate our agents and the people before the reform is put in practical operation. I fear that if we should make a mistake in this particular, we would find ourselves very much in the position that a committee of artists of New York found themselves when visiting Washington to secure the repeal of the law that places a duty on imported works of art. This committee of artists appeared before a committee of congress duly authorized to grant a hearing, and after the artists had clearly and forcibly stated their position, and backed up their request by a memorial signed by a great number of people, the Hon. H. Seed, member of congress from Seedsville, St. Lawrence County, rose from his seat, and thrusting his hands as far down into his pockets as possible, said, "Now you don't know nothing what you want. You don't want the duties taken off works of art. We know better than you what is needed, and we are going to give it to you."

Now, gentlemen, I cannot sit down without thanking the New England Insurance Exchange for the great assistance it has been to my own company during these ten active years in the business. I thank you all, friends, honestly and sincerely; and I thank you, gentlemen, for your courtesy and kindness in listening to me. [Applause.]

Mr. Goddard—I have just received a telegram from Eugene Harbeck, president of the Underwriters' Association of the Northwest:

Sincerely regretting my inability to be present at the tenth anniversary of your most valuable association, I desire, on behalf of the Northwestern association, to congratulate you on the success of your organization and the good practical work in the interest of sound underwriting which you have accomplished and are accomplishing. We extend the hand of good fellowship to you, one and all, and cordially invite you to attend our annual meeting this, the World's Fair year. If Mr. Charles Lyman Case is with you he will, as a member of our association, confirm this by word of mouth. Fraternally, EUGENE HARBECK, President.

The committee would also announce that they have received a number of letters from the managers and officers of companies and invited guests who are unable to be present with us, expressing kindly and fraternal feelings for the Exchange and their regret at their absence.

Mr. Sherman—"Boston," a beacon light whose rays of potential influence have shone on every American community, proving an important factor in moulding moral and intellectual character. We will introduce, to respond to this sentiment, a gentleman fully identified with the interests of Boston and well known in the insurance world, a self-made man, whose untiring industry, acknowledged probity, and ingenious and magnetic enterprise, have made him the sole proprietor of a leading Boston agency and the resident manager of the Imperial Fire Insurance Company. Gentlemen, Mr. John C. Paige.

REMARKS OF JOHN C. PAIGE.

Mr. Toastmaster, Mr. President and Gentlemen: A man would be insensible to the kindly feelings of his friends who was not deeply touched by such an introduction and such a greeting as you have given me here tonight. It is the more dear to me from the fact that I have been one of you, amongst you, grown up with the most of you, and am, emphatically, in my education and desires, of that grade in the profession—the highest, I think—a field man. I came into the business from the country local agency. I have always revered the local agent, but I have always honored and never forgotten the great influence, the great authority, and great usefulness of the field man. I look upon the fifteen active years of my life that I spent in the field as giving me the only real, true, genuine, foundation knowledge of the insurance business which has enabled me to get such success as I have attained. But, gentlemen, these words as regards myself, not those as regards the profession of a field man, are unpremeditated, and they have no part or lot in my response to the toast that you have given me. A larger subject, it seems to me, could not be assigned.

So long ago as the latter part of the sixteenth century, there were sturdy, well-conditioned, well-educated, forcible men in England, noted, perhaps, most chiefly for the peculiarity and sternness of their religious views—men of Lincolnshire, who were, if we read history aright, always respected but not always tolerated. They were known as "Boston men." And that, gentlemen, takes you back more than thirty years before any of those numerous small 100-ton, 30-ton and 80-ton ships came over to exploit Massachusetts and Massachusetts Bay. We find Boston in New England, established in September, 1630. We find it distinctly stated by those people who were best qualified to judge what led to the naming of Boston—we find it recorded in the diaries of Gov. Winthrop and Lieut.-Gov. Dudley that it was their intention before they left their native land to name the place in which they settled Boston. And when they arrived that somewhat singular historical character, that man who dwelt about where the Somerset club is now located, that man who at that time was the sole proprietor of the peninsula of about 900 acres which forms, with the made land, the old Boston, the actual Boston—that man, William Blackstone, living there on the side of Beacon Hill, having selected his dwelling place because of the beautiful spring located somewhere near where Louisburg square now is, and mooring his boat at the foot of what is now Pinckney street, went over to Charlestown, where Gov. Winthrop and a few of his party were temporarily quartered, and invited them to come over here and buy his land. His reason undoubtedly was that there were getting to be too many people near him. There were about 300 of these people—men, women, children, and servants—and he wanted to get away somewhere where he could worship God according to the dictates of his own conscience and not be interfered with; and so he went down into Rhode Island and established that wonderful river on which there are so many manufacturing establishments, now fully insured in the mutuals.

And, gentlemen, Boston permeated and extended and made its influence felt, and soon wiped out and obliterated the prominence of the older communities in what is now the United States of America. Its influence formed the first confederation of colonies; it created the first colonial government; in short, the colony of Massachusetts Bay became the ruling colony of the North Atlantic coast. It was the men of Boston who did this. It is due to Boston that most of the great cities of the great West and most of the railroads of the great West have been built. It is a very common thing to say that Boston neglects to look after its own and spends its entire time building up other communities. But Boston sent out some wonderful men; and touching for a moment upon the insurance business, we find it recorded that the oldest existing insurance company established in America was founded by that great Bostonian, Benjamin Franklin, born in what is now Milk street, opposite the then location of the Old South Church. It was due to the genius of Benjamin Franklin that the Philadelphia Contributionship was established. That company is still in existence, and it is fairly the oldest insurance company in America.

The first insurance company established in Boston, the Massachusetts Mutual Insurance Company, organized about 1790, was required by the law passed by the government, before it could enter upon business, to secure subscriptions amounting to $2,500,000 of fire insurance. That company was the first insurance company in Massachusetts. Prior to that time fire insurance was not known. Marine insurance was practiced by a man who kept what was called an underwriter's office, about where the Union Bank building is now located in State street. But organized insurance, the organized collection of the premiums of the many to pay the losses of the few, was first attempted in Massachusetts in 1790. At that time Boston had a population of a few thousand people. The growth of Boston was steady and the growth of the insurance business of Boston was steady. We find only as far back as the beginning of this century that the fire insurance business was so little practiced that the older Balch, the grandfather of the present president of the Boylston Insurance Company, then president of the Merchants'

Insurance Company of Boston, was accustomed to issue circulars, little sheets of paper looking very much like a small handbill, in which he pleaded with the people in curious and quaint language to come in and insure their buildings and their furniture, and their merchandise, and told them if their buildings were of a certain character the rate would be 25 cents and if they were a little worse they would be 30 cents, and if they were built entirely of wood they would be 50 cents per annum. And out of those times have grown the wonderful insurance business of the city of Boston.

But it was given to me not to talk about the insurance business of Boston, not to talk about the associations which have governed the insurance business of the city of Boston, but to say something to you of Boston in a broader and more comprehensive sense; something of that Boston which has exercised, as your toastmaster so fittingly says, a potential influence which has not been limited by the area of the United States of America; that Boston which at the time of its incorporation as a city, seventy years ago, is said by Bancroft, the historian, than whom there is no greater authority, to have been the first commercial city in the United States—more important in the commercial and manufacturing interests under its control than New York, Philadelphia, or any other city of the country; that Boston which has gone steadily forward, that Boston which has increased in population and in wealth and in potential influence, which has been built up by the people of the adjacent New England States and by the people of other countries, but which still remains exactly where we found her 270 years ago, when the Boston men came over to create a new country, to create a new life upon a new continent, when they left their homes in 1629 with the determination that they would come over here and found a town and call it Boston; that same influence, while it has not gone about the world founding other Bostons, has taken up the thread, has taken up the work of those patriots, those ancestors, those developers of this new country, and has made Boston influence everywhere felt.

We lack a little—and I say this with all knowledge of exactly what it means—we lack a little of that ecstacy which belonged to the earlier Boston and which belongs to the growing towns of the West. We are a little too much inclined to deprecate Boston. People said to me when I came here and concluded to make my residence here twenty years ago, " What do you want to throw your life away in Boston for?" Gentlemen, I appeal to you; most of you know me; has my life been thrown away trying to carve out a career in Boston? Would I have been likely to succeed better in some other town, in some town where there would have been a warmer reception to me when I came? I certainly am satisfied, and I have done what I have done in the environment of a delightful people, in a social life which is unequaled, unapproachable elsewhere than in Boston, amid surroundings which cannot be duplicated. Those old patriots, those old emigrants—for that is what they were—who came over here in 1630 and determined to found a city, founded not only a city, but they founded an influence. That influence every one of you gentlemen who reside or make your business headquarters in Boston can readily understand.

But, gentlemen, your toastmaster has admonished every one to be brief. No one ever knew me to be brief. I recollect having a head shaken at me years ago because I talked too long. But I am going to give you a few figures and not more than you can easily digest, I hope. It was in 1883 that your exchange was formed. It was in 1882 that you projected it. In 1882 the population of the city of Boston was 337,860. In 1892 it had gained more than 30 per cent and was 471,711. But, gentlemen, the valuation had gained 50 per cent and had gone up from a trifle over $600,000,000 to nearly $900,000,000. The number of mercantile buildings in the city of Boston had gained 25 per cent, and the number of dwelling houses had gained more than 30 per cent, making the total number of dwelling houses in the city limits of Boston at the present time 52,831, and a total number of buildings of 63,066, with total valuation of buildings, according to the assessors' books, of nearly $300,000,000. It is no mean city that can boast of a population within its own limits of nearly half a million and a net valuation of nearly $900,000,000, which will go probably by the assessors' valuation of next May to over $1,000,000,000. And when you take into consideration that within five miles of my office door there is a New England city just incorporated, which, in 1883, when you formed your Exchange, was a town of only 3,000 population and today has 15,000, you can see that Boston, besides growing within its municipal limits, is building up such towns and cities as Everett and others in its suburbs, while the environment of Boston gives you a total population within a radius of 11 miles of the City Hall—within a circle 22 miles in diameter—of more than 1,100,000 today. There are very few of your boom towns in the West that can match that record and show a steady increase in population and a steady increase in valuation for the whole decade.

Now, then, has Boston kept pace with the necessity of the protection of its property? Now, among the most essential elements of protection are good streets and good water works and a good fire department. The number of miles of accepted paved or macadamized streets within the city limits is now 434.59. The number of miles of water pipes, all provided with appliances making them available for fire purposes, is 557. That exceeds the number of miles of street, because of the fact that in many of the principal streets the pipes are duplicated. The increase of miles of street and miles of water pipe has been almost identical, with a slight difference in favor of the water pipes. The total capacity of the water works has increased since the Boston fire of 1872, when large expenditures were made by the then city government, from 13,000,000 gallons daily to nearly 38,000,000 at the present time, or nearly three times as much water supply as in 1872. The fire department has increased since 1872 from 101 to 603 permanent men. The number of steam fire engines in commission has increased in the same period from 21 to 43, added to which are 10 chemical engines, 23 pieces of other apparatus, such as water towers and Siamese connection, and the like, and

one fire-boat. The annual cost of maintenance of the fire department, thanks to the efforts of the Boston Board of Fire Underwriters, in which they were thoroughly supported by the mercantile community of Boston—for Boston merchants are always
patriotic in such matters when they are appealed to—has been
increased in very recent years to $1,000,000. The bulk of that
increase has been made within the last four years. In 1872 the
cost of maintenance of the Boston fire department was in round
numbers $400,000, and in 1882 it had only advanced to $460,000,
whereas in 1892 the appropriation for the current expenses of
the fire department for the municipal year, as I have said, was
$1,000,000.

Gentlemen, you must see that those underwriters of Boston who
are members of that—in your minds—somewhat halting institution, the Boston Board of Fire Underwriters, have accomplished a
good deal in the little baliwick of a few hundred acres which is
under their control. Fire insurance premiums of the city of Boston
have increased in the last ten years very much more in proportion
than the valuation. The valuation, as I have already told you,
has increased, substantially, 40 per cent, and the fire insurance
premiums have increased, substantially, 50 per cent. The
amount of fire losses, I am sorry to say—but it is necessary to
say it in order to show that we have not imposed upon the public
—has increased in the same ratio. There is no more probability
of making money upon the rates of today for the fire insurance
companies than there was upon the rates of 1892. The Exchange
and the Boston Board of Fire Underwriters were born within a
few weeks of each other. The Boston Board of Fire Underwriters, then called the Boston Tariff Association, came into
being about two months earlier than the Exchange But it
came into being, gentlemen, at a time when the Boston underwriting interests were in a very healthy condition; 1882, I
believe, the secretary of the Boston board will tell you when he
comes to speak—and far be it from me to use up his functions—
was about the most profitable year that the fire insurance companies ever had in Boston. And yet they organized an associa-

tion which has done all of this work in anticipation of bad times to come, because they saw all about them in New England that there were bad times, and they knew it was simply because of some peculiar fortune that Boston was not in bad condition at the same time that its associates and neighbors were in bad condition.

But, gentlemen, I now want to ask you one thing more. I conceived it was my duty to come here and talk up Boston. I am not native; I am not to the manor born, although I am a New Englander by birth. I know that the great bulk of the people in the city of Boston were not born in Boston, but I know that the newcomers, the *emigres*, so to speak, are as loyal to the city and as hearty in its support as are its own children. I only want to say to you now, gentlemen, that when you go out into the field to talk about your business, it seems only fair, only what it is for your self-interest to do—and I know of nothing more likely to govern men in their actions than self-interest—it is nothing more than what it is your self-interest to do, to preach Boston, to advocate Boston, to indicate to everyone with whom you come in contact that Boston is a great and growing and flourishing city, into which they want to pour all of their savings and to which they want to come with all their business—not insurance business, but other business. The Boston people are entirely satisfied with what insurance business naturally belongs in Boston, but they want you to go out and talk up Boston. They do not want you to try the effect as you go about of acting towards Boston as a man does when he tries to wink at a pretty woman in the dark.

Mr. Sherman—"The Special Agent." There is no more arduous, or delicate, or responsible position connected with a fire insurance company than that occupied by the faithful special agent, and when he enjoys the fullest confidence of his principals in his ubiquitous duties, he makes or he mars the reputation of his company in the field over which he is supervisor. All honor to the loyal special agent. We are exceedingly fortunate in being able to introduce to you as a respondent to this toast one who from several years' successful experience, both as special agent in the field and supervisor of field work in the home office, is fully competent to address us understandingly on this subject. Gentlemen, the secretary of the Old Ætna Insurance Company.

REMARKS OF JAMES F. DUDLEY.

Gentlemen: The special agent is entitled to a much abler advocate than you have in me tonight, and it is a matter of regret that the president was not able to produce someone who could better do justice to you than I can. My only apology for accepting the position and allowing myself to be put to the front in this matter is the intense interest that I have in you and my great respect for you, which has grown up from having served many years in the field together with you and knowing fully and well the arduous duties which are daily placed upon you.

I have but one or two thoughts to express tonight, as we have all lived the same life and have had the same experiences with our trials and our triumphs, so that I could do nothing more except repeat in other words what you perhaps already could better than I can and know as fully as myself. Some years ago, at one of the large meetings of the national board as a rate-making power—I believe the body still lives—when the fact that rates could not be made by companies and maintained became admitted, although, as it seemed then, a sorrowful fact, a body of gentlemen representing the New York State field men appeared on the floor of the convention and modestly asked that the experiment might be entrusted to them of making the rates in New York State. The matter, of course, in the light of the history of the Exchange, seems absurd, but suffice it to say that the very proposition met with the most violent opposition from a number of leading underwriters. One gentleman, prominent then in insurance circles, as he is today, was especially pronounced in his opposition. Present then as I was, as a young special agent, the remark that he made left a lasting impression on my memory. Quoting after the lapse of years, he said something like this: "No man has a higher regard for special agents than I; no man will sing louder pæans to the worth of a special agent than I; but before I will consent that the special agents shall make rates for my company, I will resign my position."

Gentlemen, he has never resigned. Ten years of your history has shown that the rate-making power has been entrusted to the specials of New England, and the highest compliment that could be paid to your success lies in the fact that the entire territory east of that controlled by the Western Union, and north of that controlled by the Southeastern Tariff Association—throughout that entire territory the only rate-making power today is, in fact, the special agent, with the exception, I should say, of a few cities. We presume, gentlemen, that none of you have laid claim to infallibility in your work. It is happy for us that such has been the fact with you, for were it otherwise we presume that you would all be, today, at the Vatican and not here in New England and we enjoying your services.

But this rate-making power, which up to that time was an unknown quantity in the special agent, and now has become so common and so much a matter of course that it seems almost a matter of ancient history to refer to it, is by no means the only element that makes up the constituency of the special agent. In your fits of modesty,.gentlemen, did you ever investigate yourselves and see the variety of phases which you present? It sometimes seems to me that as you turn the kaleidoscope, and at every moment new forms appear, so in the multitude of work and the variety of duties thrown upon the special agent, at every turn of the special agent you discover new elements which are prominent in his character. And as the crystal from every face flashes a new gleam of light, it seems to me that the special, called upon as he is today to occupy so many positions, from each new position he assumes displays a new ability. The commissioner has well spoken of the enormous strides with which our business has advanced. We have to admit that of the great number of thousands of dollars paid in New England, it is almost entirely paid through your hands. Upon your good judgment or your failure in judgment, as it may be, depend frequently the most unpleasant lawsuits and the most troublesome litigations into which companies are thrown. And to your own good judgment in the settlement of so many cases is due the fact that so few lawsuits do occur.

Again, I do not know that the special agent has ever disputed with nature her axiom that two bodies cannot occupy the same space at a given time; but from my observation of men in that capacity I know you have endeavored frequently to demonstrate the fact that one body can occupy two spaces at the same time. The special, today, is here adjusting a loss, tomorrow, with the stride of a Bluebeard, he is on the outskirts of New York State adjusting the accounts of an insolvent agent before the other fellow gets there. The special agent, too, is supposed to be the embodiment of all information. Of values you are supposed to estimate with accuracy from that of a cambric needle to a saw mill. You are supposed to be familiar with all the processes of chemistry. You are supposed to know all methods of manufacture, from the burning of lime to the composition of nitro-glycerine, and there is no compound that is so intricate as is not supposed to be within your ken, from the component parts of Ayer's sarsaparilla to the mysteries of an early hotel breakfast in the country.

But, gentlemen, brevity is required of us all. To do justice to the qualities of a special agent and the fidelity with which he discharges his duties would require more than a ten minutes' speech. The rate-making power of your association has been supplemented lately by a duty which I may safely say is the most important ever assumed by any underwriters' organization. You have lately assumed the role of a legislator, and by the promulgation of the co-insurance clause, which has gone forth from your halls within a few days, you have taken a new departure, which is the most pronounced and upon which we look with the most interest as to its successful termination of anything which has characterized your history. And it is with great interest that we watch the results that shall accrue from that measure. You remember in the wandering of Ulysses that Circe told him that in his crafts he must avoid on the left Charybdis, which in venturing too near would swallow him up, or in approaching too near to the right to Scylla he would have seizures made which would greatly deplete his numbers. Now, gentlemen, in the course of your legislation in the new role which you have assumed, remember that there is no position which so imperatively requires a steady compass and straight sailing as that of the legislator. On the one hand you have to contend against what seems to be ruin to your companies; on the other hand you come within the grasp of that jealous public which is ever watchful of our actions.

But, gentlemen, this topic is exhaustive; it is more than is allowed for a few minutes speech; it calls for more than the opportunities of a mere response to a toast will allow me to say and still do justice to you. I should certainly be oblivious to fifteen of the happiest years of my life in which I served as a field man, associated closely and most happily with many of you who are assembled about this table tonight, and whose bounty we have accepted, and for whom I shall gratefully express my recognition, did I not have a high regard for the special agents of New England. It has properly been said that from Boston has emanated much that has been of great service to the world. It might be properly said that from Boston emanated the first ideas to people which have influenced the good of others. It is fitting, then, that in Boston the sessions of the New England Insurance Exchange should convene from week to week; that from those sessions should go forth to other similar bodies throughout the country an example showing a careful discrimination in what is in the interests of our business, which is mature and can be properly followed by others. And sitting as you do tonight almost within the shadow of the old belfry from which glimmered the lantern of Paul Revere, throwing intelligence to those beyond, it is fitting that from your association, convening from week to week in Boston, should emanate a halo which in itself should reflect upon the intelligence of the New England special agents constituting the New England Insurance Exchange.

Mr. Sherman—" The Insurance Library Association " of Boston, an indispensable adjunct in advancing our exchange work and promoting our individual interests, an institution that is worthy of our hearty encouragement and earnest support. It gives me pleasure to introduce to this assembly the president of the Insurance Library Association of Boston, and one of the vice-presidents of the New England Insurance Exchange, Mr. Frederick B. Carpenter.

REMARKS OF F. B. CARPENTER.

Mr. President and Gentlemen : In behalf of the Insurance Library Association of Boston, which I have the honor to represent, I thank you cordially. As the membership of the Insurance Library Association of Boston and the New England Insurance Exchange is virtually the same, there is very little that I can say to the members. But I take this opportunity, Mr. President, to add to your welcome to the honored guests here assembled this evening by inviting them to do us the honor of a personal visit to our library rooms during their stay in the city. Gentlemen, your presence will cheer us and the trustees will give you a hearty welcome. I thank you, gentlemen.

Mr. Sherman—" The New England Bureau of United Inspection," its intelligent and efficient work its highest commendation. We will introduce as respondent to this toast an honorary member of our Exchange, a gentleman whose uniform courtesy and urbanity while an active member and president of our organization won our universal respect and esteem, and whose promotion to the managerial chair excited not our envy but strengthened our personal regard and personal admiration. A gentleman whose business career in our midst well illustrates the truth of one of Solomon's proverbs: "The hand of the diligent shall bear rule" Mr. George P. Field, president of the organization which we have toasted and one of the managers for New England of the Royal Insurance Company.

REMARKS OF GEORGE P. FIELD.

Mr. Toastmaster: So far as the very flattering introduction you give me applies to the organization I represent, I accept it. So far as it applies to me individually, I feel very much as I imagine that small boy did when he went down with his father to get an overcoat and heard the salesman tell the father that "the coat vas a shplendid fit, but the tam boy vas too shmall."

I am here tonight not only in my capacity as the chairman of the governing committee of the New England Bureau of United Inspection—a most sonorous title, I want you to understand that —but also as a kicker. I am not going to try to ring in on you that old moth-eaten chestnut that I didn't expect to be called upon and am not prepared, because I have got a most beautiful oration, typewritten, in my pocket, like these other gentlemen. But before I deliver it I want to make a little personal explanation. When this "debauch" was finally determined upon and the beautiful four-sheet posters were sent out, I was waited upon by the governing committee and told that I was to attend as an ex-president of the association and that I was to respond to a sentiment in regard to the associations and memories that linger around the ten years of our organization—a kind of a Mark Antony address over lots of dead Cæsars. Well, I expended a good deal of gray matter in getting up that oration. The eulogies of the departed members would have brought tears to the eyes of the waiters; the eulogies on those of you who are alive the most hardened old jester in the "gang" would blush to read.

But just as I got that done, enter the committee; they had found that they had gone long on ex-presidents but they were mighty short on managers of kindred organizations, and they would run me in as chairman of the inspection bureau or president of the protective. Well, the latter was a soft snap, because I have a speech as the president of the protective department that is a perfect daisy. The last time I delivered it, at the Revere House, before the Barnicoat Veterans, I brought down the house and a quantity of crockery at the same time off from the sideboard, against which some one was leaning.

But as chairman of the bureau I never have had occasion to speak, and I started out on a lot of statistics. I was going to show you the percentage of sprinkled risks to unsprinkled risks, the percentage of loss per sprinkler head in the United States, the percentage of risks that we inspect that don't burn, and lots of other things. I got pretty well along, and it occurred to me if I could get some figures from the mutuals for comparative purposes it would be a grand, good idea. So I went up into the temple on Milk street and interviewed the high priest, Hon. Edward Atkinson, president of the Boston Manufacturers' Mutual, and told him what I was going to do, and he said, "Don't. When I was a young man I had a little leaning towards statistics, and I wrote two or three papers, and finally one of them was criticised, and the conclusion of the critic was this: 'There are lies, and d—d lies, and statistics.' So," he said, "if I were in your place I wouldn't tackle it in the superlative degree." And I thought he was about right, and the consequence was that that speech I was going to make to you I am going to publish as my annual report of the inspection bureau, and you gentlemen can all read it when you are sober, and it will do you a great deal more good than it would tonight.

But there is one thing that I do want to say in all seriousness as a Boston underwriter, as one whose interests are entirely in New England, who has been, I may say, one of the charter members of the Exchange and somewhat prominently identified with its earlier career, and that is to thank these gentlemen from abroad who have left their desks at this very busy time in the year to come here and be with us, because it can only be taken as an expression of the confidence they feel in the work of the

Exchange and as an evidence of good will towards us. I know myself how hard it is; we are all of us overwhelmed with work in the attempt to answer those irrelevant conundrums that my bald-headed old friend over there (Commissioner Merrill) with the other commissioners of the various states fire at us at this time of the year, and it really means a great deal for these gentleman to come from these other cities over here to meet the New England Insurance Exchange, and I most cordially thank them, as I know you all do. And now, Mr. President, incidentally remarking that if you have found out anything about the New England Bureau of Inspection, it is not my fault, I am done.

Mr. Sherman —"The Insurance Press," the handmaid of insurance, its safest guide, its strongest friend, and its most earnest and loyal ally. The press is a wonderful diffuser and promoter of popular intelligence, and the great Webster once said, "The intelligence of the people is the security of society." To respond to this sentiment we will call upon a gentleman who needs no introduction, our friend, the editor of THE STANDARD, Col. C. M. Ransom of Boston.

REMARKS OF C. M. RANSOM.

Gentlemen: I congratulate myself on the good fortune which enables me to be with you this evening and desire to express my thanks, both for the privilege and pleasure of participating in this intellectual feast and in the good cheer which prevails around this fraternal and hospitable board, and in which all present seem most cordially to join in properly celebrating the tenth anniversary of one of the most intelligently managed and most successful underwriting organizations, considering its scope, in our land—the New England Insurance Exchange.

The advance in individual life is, in our thoughts, marked by decades, so too, is it noted in domestic life, and in a public way the growth of municipal life—state and national—is chronicled by comparison by decades. Following this rule it is highly appropriate that this body should celebrate its first decade—its tin wedding—in this delightful and interesting manner, and my first thought comes to me in words of congratulation and satisfaction in the prosperity of the past, and the future promises for good which are foretold by this assemblage on this anniversary night.

The success of the New England Insurance Exchange is due to the tact, good judgment, patient perseverance, and marked ability of its members, and to the intelligent performance of their duties are we indebted for the greatly improved condition of the business of fire underwriting in New England, as well as for the pace they have set for fire underwriters in other sections of the country. It is but just and proper, then, in view of this public service that you gentlemen, the officers and managers of fire insurance companies represented in this field, and coming from different sections, should lend the encouraging sanction of your presence on this occasion in honorable recognition of the good results that have been accomplished by your servants. But I am straying from the subject assigned me—the Insurance Press—and trust you will pardon this brief digression.

It is always a pleasure to speak of the press, in any of its multifarious and important relations to society for its common good, and on this occasion I desire to speak of it as it should be from my point of observation. The general press should be the intelligent leader of public sentiment toward a better and a higher civilization ; the educator of the young in all those nobler elements which constitute good citizenship ; the sentinel upon the outer wall to warn community of approaching political or social dangers ; the power, when occasion requires, which can make or unmake men and nations ; the shield and protector of the law-abiding citizen, and a terror to the evil-doer, hence, only men with pure hearts and clean hands, men of the highest character and noblest impulses should direct and control its utterances. All these high moral attributes and requirements of the general press belong by right to the insurance press, in its varied and responsible relations to insurance, and its teachings and practices should be such as to commend it not only to the underwriting fraternity, but to the public as well; in brief, it should be the handmaid of insurance, its safest guide, its strongest friend, and its most earnest and loyal ally. It should be an independent press, devoted exclusively to its legitimate field, commending when commendation is deserved, and criticising in a dignified, friendly, but impressive manner whenever and wherever such criticism will advance the best interests of insurance, without in any way being influenced by fear or favor, since a just and fair criticism is always for the best interests of any association or business, while an unfair and uncalled for criticism is never justified under any circumstances. Its expressions should be able, fearless, and at the same time considerate of the feelings, sentiments, and interests of others, and above all it should be high minded, always truthful, and should never fail to appreciate the responsible duties of its high vocation.

In order to meet these essential requirements each member of the insurance press should be a walking encyclopedia of insurance lore, ever active in seeking the latest news, data, and information for the enlightenment and guidance of those engaged in the great, growing, and important business of underwriting, and while he seeks in a modest, unassuming way to instruct his readers in correct principles and practices, and to warn them against the opposite, he should at the same time seek to build up, and not destroy, the cause he is in duty bound to protect and perpetuate. As in olden times the beacon lights on the mountain tops flashed out their signals for the guidance of the people in the valley, so should the insurance press lighten the pathway of all engaged in this wide-extended, exacting, and honorable business. Personalities engendered by ill feeling, jealousy, or spite should have no part or place in its columns, nor should encouragement be given to stirring up strife and animosity among companies and agents. The true sentiment which should prevail with all its members, as well as with the members of your fraternity, is most fittingly illustrated by the following lines from Sheldon:

" In sweet'ning the life of another,
In relieving a *brother's* distress,
The *soul* finds it *highest* advancement,
And the *noblest* blessedness.

That life is alone worth the living
That lives for *another's* gain,
The life that comes after *such* living,
Is the rainbow after the rain."

Gentlemen, let us set our mark high, and strive in accordance with these noble sentiments to sweeten the lives of others, and thus obtain a full view of the rainbow after the rain. In order that the insurance press can be fully equipped to best serve the interests of the cause it advocates, it should be respected, recognized, and encouraged by those whom its mission is to serve. As between members of the insurance fraternity and those of the insurance press, there should exist the utmost confidence; counsel should be freely sought and as freely given by each, since each, if honest to his calling, to community, and himself, is striving to accomplish the same desirable result—the greatest good to the greatest number.

This may not be the day of an ideal insurance press, but both observation and experience furnish unmistakable evidence that we are much nearer that goal than we were a decade ago. To it has come better thought and better practices, and more midnight oil is being consumed in a closer study of the science and intricacies of insurance in all its branches than in the past, and while we have not, and never may reach the millenium in our profession, we are still improving, and our progress along that line we sincerely trust will be constantly accelerated and not in any way impeded. The history of the insurance press has become the history of insurance; the two are so intimately interwoven with each other that the growth and progress of one has become the synonym of strength and prosperity of both.

What the insurance press most needs, gentlemen, is, I repeat, your respect, your confidence, and your encouragement for still higher and nobler aims; your condemnation of the wrong, and your commendation of the right in its practices; its full recognition as your co-laborer in the great field of insurance, and the free bestowment of your best and wisest counsel. Then, and not till then, will it be prepared to render to your profession its best and highest service. In closing, please permit me to quote, as equally applicable to you and me, in our future life work, this beautiful sentiment of the late poet, the sainted Whittier:

> " We shape ourselves the joy or fear,
> Of which the coming life is made,
> And fill our future atmosphere
> With sunshine or with shade.
>
> The tissue of the life to be
> We weave with colors all our own,
> And in the field of destiny
> We reap as we have sown."

Mr. Sherman—" Insurance Companies and Their Agents." The local agent is a mighty factor in the conduct of our business and on no one element are its successful and satisfactory results more dependent. I am much pleased to introduce a gentleman of extended experience in the home office of a leading agency company, who is well qualified to speak wisely and well to this toast, Mr. J. H. Washburn, vice-president of the Home Insurance Company of New York.

REMARKS OF J. H. WASHBURN.

Mr. President, Mr. Toastmaster, and Gentlemen: It is unfortunate for me that you have short memories. If you had remembered with what a large auger I bored this New England Exchange at their dinner nine years ago, I am sure you never would have asked me to repeat the dose. But you appear to have forgotten, for you have asked me to come again. I hate to write and I don't keep a typewriter ; the consequence is, I haven't any written speech, and you must take what you can get.

Horace Greeley wrote two big volumes to tell what he didn't know about farming. If I were to tell you all I do know about insurance companies and agents, I am afraid your toastmaster would call me down long before I got through, for I have had a very long acquaintance with both. Let me say first, I believe there is no class of corporations where integrity has been more noted and where a failure of integrity has been more seldom noticed than in the insurance companies of this country. Let me say further, I know of no class of men representing the interests of others far away from them, under not the master's eye, far away from the reach of the home office, where those interests have been so faithfully cared for, where there has been less occasion for complaint of the misuse of the powers entrusted to the agent than we find among the thousands of insurance agents throughout our land.

There are many things in that direction which I might say. But I want to say one word about the relations which do exist and should exist between the companies and their agents. If the golden rule were the guide of all our lives, there would be no question what those relations are or should be. If we all, at both ends of the line, remembered that our interests are common, that there can be nothing for the lasting interest of the agent that is not for the interest of the company, there would be no occasion for misunderstandings between agents and their companies. But we are human, Mr. President; we can all make mistakes. We can all forget that in seeking the interests of our principal we are promoting our own. We are too apt to look in a small circle at what is close to us and forget the great and lasting interests; and out of that grows the misunderstanding, grow all the difficulties that arise between the corporations and their agents.

As between agents themselves, misunderstandings occasionally arise. They lap over sometimes and tread on one another's toes. An old divine once, in speaking of the differences between the various denominations of Christians, said that as he went about among his people he found there was nothing that so contributed to good neighborhood among the farmers as a strong five-rail fence. I believe that nothing is better calculated to promote and conserve friendly relations between companies and their agents than thoroughly to define their fields, cutting them apart by that strong five-rail fence, and never allowing a trespass in that field. And I would say that the same practice should exist as between the companies themselves and their agents: they should not tread on an agent's toes, nor write a risk over his head.

If agents would remember that as a rule their experience is in a limited field, in a limited class of business, that their principals survey the whole field and have the benefit of a long and large and wide experience and may reasonably be expected to judge more carefully and correctly of the character of the business desirable for them to write than the agent can possibly do from his limited point of view, they would be less restive under the criticisms they receive; they would remember that the company furnishing the capital, paying the losses, bearing all the responsibility, knowing best what the character of the business is and should be, can judge better how the risk should be written and what should be written and when and how much and on what terms, they would less often subject themselves to unpleasant criticisms. Each company has its own standard, and after a little each agent comes to learn what his company wants, and an agent who is wise and judicious and desires to maintain pleasant relations with his principal will be careful how he offers or forces upon his company risks which, however desirable they seem to him, however desirable he knows they may be to some other companies, he has reason to believe are distasteful and regarded as undesirable by any one company whose policy he wishes to write.

Some agents have a way—you all know how it is—there are some risks that these agents have that we get to know as "rounders." They will be offered to one company and then refused. The policy will be cancelled and placed in another company, and so sometimes insurance will be given on the most undesirable risk in an agent's field in every company he has, running over weeks and perhaps months, for which no company receives any compensation and for which each in turn carries an undesirable responsibility. Is that fair treatment of the companies? And yet you all know that that is done repeatedly. There is one link between companies and their agents upon which their relations and their character largely depend. That link you, gentlemen, in this field supply. The special agent of the company is the connecting link between the agent and his company, and upon his character, upon his manner, upon his method of treating the agents, upon the mode in which he discharges his duty, rests much of the character of the relation between the companies and the agents. It is pleasant to stand here and look you in the face and say that as far as I know, and my experience is pretty wide, there is no group of special agents anywhere who discharge that duty of making pleasant relations between companies and agents better than those who are represented in the New England Insurance Exchange.

Now, one word only. I want to take down a little bit of the boasting that I hear here. Boston is the centre of a great many things. From it a great many things originate. But New York is not entirely behind in originating good things. The first organization of underwriters, the first attempt at schedule rating, was not in Boston but in the city of New York, much as you may say of Boston's influence in that direction. Away back before many of us—yes, I think before any of us had much to do with underwriting—there was more than one convention held in New York, and rate books and schedule rates were issued by a conference of companies gathered together, which are the basis and the foundation of our ratings today. And good as the work of the New England Insurance Exchange has been, early as it was in the field, the Western Underwriters' Association antedates it. As a rating institution it has passed its usefulness, but still maintains its organization, and is today a useful disseminator of insurance knowledge. There is in the West an association which is a rating organization, which is a power throughout the States where it exerts its influence, which by some years antedates the New England Exchange, and that is the Union—today perhaps as powerful an organization for good for underwriters as any that exists in the country. I say not this to detract at all from the merit of the Exchange, but as a representative of the Union, as one who was honored by being for more than two terms its president, I cannot allow you to claim the honor of being the first of the present existing organizations of the kind in this country.

And now, gentlemen, let me say one word more, and I am through. I won't tax you too long, Mr. Toastmaster. There is nothing in my judgment that does more to promote the pleasant relations which should exist between companies and their agents than gatherings like this tonight. When we meet and break bread together and look one another in the face, we do much to cement those relations which should exist between us. We do more, I believe, than we can do in any other way. And for this reason I thank you, gentlemen, for inviting me to be present tonight. It has given me great pleasure to meet you and to look into your faces.

Mr. Sherman—"Underwriters and the Insuring Public." The interests of the insuring public and the companies are identical. The better the mutual understanding, the greater the mutual confidence. We are pleased to introduce to respond to this sentiment a gentleman of New England parentage and culture, the able and genial president of the Phenix Insurance Company of New York, Mr. George P. Sheldon.

REMARKS OF GEORGE P. SHELDON.

Mr. President, Mr. Toastmaster, and Gentlemen: If the public at large could have been brought here tonight and could have listened to the sentiments that have been expressed here, if they could have listened to the record of the work of this organization, if they could have heard the feelings expressed here of the responsibility felt for yourselves in the work in which you have been engaged for ten years; if even next to that, they could have a transcript presented to them which would faithfully express the spirit, not alone of this gathering, but of your work during this ten years, it would not be necessary in any formal way to speak to the sentiment which has been assigned to me, of the relations of underwriters and the insuring public.

I look back with great pleasure to my first introduction to the New England Insurance Exchange. It is the first underwriting organization that I had the pleasure of being presented to, and from that introduction I have followed the work of the Exchange very closely through the past five years. It seems to me that at the foundation of your work you started on the right track when you were ready to disseminate information—information which would be valuable to the public at large and enable them to understand better than they had understood before these relations which exist between them and the underwriting companies. I think that the work that you have done here in this field during the past ten years has accomplished more in bringing together the companies and the public than has been done in any other field, so far as my knowledge goes. As you have come face to face with the parties to whom you have delivered policies from time to time, as you have discussed with them from your intelligent standpoint the relations that exist and which suggest to you the business contract that finally results between the company and the insured, you have dissipated all the prejudices and many of the misapprehensions that have resulted in the unfortunate, unjust and disastrous legislation which prevails throughout many departments. If there is one spirit that has prevailed here in this field it seems to me it is the spirit of co-operation.

As one listened here tonight to the history of the organization of this Exchange, he could not have failed of being impressed with the great influence of that spirit when this Exchange started. You felt the need of one another's help, and you at the same time recognized the fact that, differences as there were between you, there were principles upon which you could unite and engage together in this work. And when once that spirit of co-operation was firmly established among yourselves, the next step was to extend that same co-operation from the underwriters to the public. One step naturally suggested the other, and when the first was taken it was comparatively easy to take the second. Why is it, that when you decide to establish the principle of co-insurance there is scarcely a ripple all through your field, the community at large saying, after the education that they have had at your hands for so many years, " We recognize the voice of this Exchange; we have known them and watched their work during these years; we believe that this principle expresses their best judgment, looking not simply at the interest of the companies, but looking at the interests of the public as well; and, having that confidence in their judgment, we accept this principle of co-insurance; we will adopt it, cause it to enter into our relations with the companies, and we believe that it will result in good, not simply to the companies, but also to the community at large."

The honored commissioner of the Massachusetts insurance department has referred to this enormous loss that has come upon the companies during the past two years. Now, if those facts in regard to the terrible losses could be spread abroad in the same spirit that they were referred to here tonight, by the officers of similar departments throughout the country, that of itself would be a very valuable assistance to us in our business. It is our duty to furnish this information; it is our duty to call attention to the fact, as has been so well expressed by him, that the companies are merely the distributors of the premiums contributed by the insured, and that if they are to have security and indemnity furnished by the companies, why, the companies have got to collect just so much from them; they have, therefore, the principal interest in doing what they can to reduce and to eliminate these enormous losses. Now when we explain the matter in this way, when we show to them that according as these losses run premiums must be secured, then will they, possibly not cheerfully at first, but when their intelligent judgment acts they will accept the suggestions as to what the proper rates should be.

Now reference has been made here from time to time to the work in New York; I feel very much as the last speaker does in regard to that. While appreciating the great work that has been done here, there is work also done from New York as a centre. The headquarters of the national board, which has been referred to so often here tonight, are in New York City. From those headquarters there is going out all the while the most valuable information, throughout New England, throughout the Middle States, throughout the South, throughout the West—information collected by the companies represented through the national board. The information when it is collected is not concealed in the archives of that venerable institution; it is sent out, not only to the companies, the members, but where the improvements referred to are sought to be accomplished; the requirements are submitted to the proper officials in the various cities and towns that have been examined by our inspector and they form the basis for the results that we want to accomplish there. Until they know the defects in a general way, they will not move to correct them.

Sometimes it is necessary to bring them up sharply, to call public attention in an abrupt way to these deficiencies, as was lately done in a neighboring city to New York; and what was the result? The mayor of that city asked if a committee of underwriters would meet with him and consult as to these defects. His invitation was promptly accepted and the honored vice-president of the Home Insurance Company, in an interview which did not last many minutes, gave that official, the head of the city, the mayor, the chief of the fire department, the principal committee of the city council, and some of the most influential citizens, more information with regard to the condition of that city, with reference to its water supply, its fire department, its equipment, and to the personnel of the force, than apparently all of them together had ever conceived of before. When that interview was sought there was that large gathering of people whose views had been reported in the public press before in condemnation of the underwriters for insisting on a 25 per cent advance of certain classes of risks in the city of Brooklyn; but since that interview was held, a few days ago, the tone of the press in that city has entirely changed, and the condemnation is not now towards the underwriters, but they are asking their officials there, "Why do these things exist?" When once we establish such relations as that with municipalities, the way is open for an intelligent adjustment of the relations between such a community and the underwriters.

One of the other subjects that I would like to refer to very briefly—it has been suggested by the invitation extended to me as the president of the commission compact—is the item of expense of doing our business. It it not necessary for us to dwell long on that subject. I think that we would all admit that for the past ten or twelve years expenses have been increasing at a rate not at all warranted by the relations existing between the underwriters and the insuring public. It became necessary for an organization to be effected to arrest that movement, and when once an organization was effected to arrest it, they found it could not be arrested except by taking back track. And when the companies through their executive officers came to consider the matter, they were compelled by the necessity of the situation to look it squarely in the face and to say that not only must it be checked where it was, but that, recognizing that the business could stand only an expense of 15 per cent as a commission to an agent, that must be the basis for the future and the only safe basis for the company to stand upon. Now, gentlemen, I am very glad to stand here tonight and to recognize the help and assistance the companies have had through your membership, through you as individuals, in bringing about this great reform. But we shall fail yet of our duty if we stop there. We believe that more yet can be done in the way of reducing expenses and thus enable us to justify ourselves and put ourselves in a position to re-establish the public in our confidence or to re-establish ourselves in the confidence of the public; to bring about that mutual relation which we all want, which will enable us to secure an adequate return for the policies we issue, enabling the companies to be strong, at the same time to be just.

I do not propose to refer to any further details about that tonight, but simply suggest this: among the items of information that the public are entitled to have is a plain statement of the condition of companies. We have learned for a number of years to rest the condition of the company entirely upon its formal reports to the departments established in the various states. They are good so far as they go. There are organizations that have not been required in some states, at least, even to formally report to the departments their condition, but are satisfied to go before the insuring public pledging their ability to pay whatever losses may be actually incurred, and beyond that, recognizing no obligation on their part to give any information whatever to the public. We all know that a company that is doing business must not only be prepared to pay what losses may accrue, but also must be prepared to return to the living policies the portion of premium which we say is unearned. Now there are companies, there are associations that seem to lose sight of the fact that it is necessary to have an unearned premium fund; and when they go to the assured and present their policy and submit to them propositions for their business, they forget to set forth this fact. Now, is that just to the public? Is that just to the companies that are represented around these tables, that are obliged to set forth to the last detail all the particulars of their business? Will the insuring public long submit to take the policies of such organizations and be satisfied with only the insufficient information which is given out in regard to what is back of them? Have we any duty to perform in that particular? I submit the matter for your consideration, leaving it here, standing for myself, standing, I believe, for the stock underwriting interests, when I say that recognizing our obligation to make this full and explicit statement, we have the right to demand of others that they shall do the same.

Gentlemen, as I look into your faces here tonight, it is an inspiration for the future. If the same intelligence is to be expended in the future that has been in the past and on the same lines, when we gather here, as I hope we all may, ten years from now, and look one another again in the face, if there are any misapprehensions or misunderstandings now existing between underwriters and the insuring public, I feel that by that time they will have all disappeared and that there will be such a co-operation as has never been seen in this country, each, the insurer and the insured, recognizing their mutual obligations and responsibilities to each other.

Mr. Emerson—Gentlemen, it has been suggested that some of our venerable friends who sit at the other end of the hall would perhaps feel like leaving, but we hope they will remain with the boys at this end, who propose to stay, for the best wine always comes last. It is thought best to omit the next song and proceed with the programme.

Mr. Sherman—" Schedule Rating," the only scientific basis for the fixing of the premiums by fire underwriters. The inception of all great improvements in any enterprise has usually had its origin in the agitation engendered and persistently promoted by some one individual, who has often been called a " crank " and his favored object a " hobby " In the end, however, the individual has been endorsed and his scheme adopted. We have with us, as one of our guests this evening, a gentleman, perhaps we should say *the* gentleman, who has for many years made a special study of the plan of schedule rating, and has been the central figure in the discussion concerning it. He is abundantly able to entertain us on this important subject. Gentlemen, the president of the Continental Fire Insurance Company, Mr. F. C. Moore.

REMARKS OF F. C. MOORE.

Mr. Toastmaster, Mr. President, and Gentlemen: I esteem it a great privilege to speak before such a body of men. I esteem it a great honor that the New England Insurance Exchange thinks it worth while to listen to what I have to say.

And the first thing I have to say is this: That throughout nine years of the decade which marks the history of this organization, I have entertained but one opinion, and that is that it is the most practical and able underwriting organization in the United States. The territory which you have in charge is a peculiar one. It embraces, I believe, every known hazard, excepting, possibly, quartz mills and cotton gins, and I could not pay a higher compliment than this—nor could I say anything that would demonstrate the truth that I have claimed for the association more than this—that with such splendid opportunities of learning all the phases of this business, you have made the best use of them.

It is especially fitting that before the New England Exchange I, as one of the schedule committee, should be first called upon to say anything about it, because it is my pleasant duty to say tonight that but for the hearty co-operation of the New England Insurance Exchange the universal schedule would not be what it is. The New England Exchange, of all the rating organizations of the country, first responded to the call for help. One of the ablest men that we could have had on that small original committee of four—a man who never shirked any of the hard work connected with the task—was a member of the New England Insurance Exchange, Mr. Richards of Hartford. The first committee appointed as a co-operating committee was that of the New England Exchange, and in point of numbers it outnumbers any other. And at that first meeting held in Hartford, which lasted three days and nights, I think, of the hottest weather I ever experienced, that New England Exchange committee was there, man for man, and on the only occasion when, I may modestly state, the chairman of the universal committee was a few minutes late, the chairman of the New England Exchange committee, Mr. Henry R. Turner, was present and called the roll, and the only response was from a member of the New England Exchange, Mr. Henry R. Turner, and I have the best evidence of the fact from his own lips.

In the brief time allotted to me — for I shall not disregard the admonition of the toastmaster — I shall have little opportunity to go into the consideration of any detail, and I shall be of necessity compelled to deal with generalities. I want to say this for that schedule: that whether it be right or wrong—and the men who have had the making of it believe it is very nearly right today—this we do claim, that the process of framing it which we followed was the only correct process to get a correct schedule; for we called to our aid the counsel, the advice, the knowledge and the experience of the men of the continent, and we sent every proof of that schedule, so far as I was able to collect the names of the underwriters of the country, to every special agent of every company, to every officer of every company, and to many of the practical local agents of the country, and we had suggestions from Maine to California, and from England as well. Now, gentlemen, it has been said that that schedule will reduce rates. So it will. If it did not reduce some rates in this country, it would be the best evidence that it was not right nor worth listening to. But it raises rates as well, and it hopes and expects to do this: that it shall not charge the faults of one man's risk on another man's risk that has not faults.

It has been conceded by critics that it was at least educational. Indeed it is. For myself I would not take thousands of dollars for the education it was to me to get the benefit of the judgment and advice of men throughout the country on all the subjects of which that schedule treats. It has been a fish net, with meshes so fine that it drew out the opinions of men on every subject connected with the construction of a building, the cost of a fire or its extinction. Now, gentlemen, I have observed this fact: that I entered upon that task with well settled ideas on matters which I thought unimportant: I should never have asked any man his opinion about them. And but for this process, this fish net, so to speak, which drew out their opinions, I never would have gotten them, and I would have died in ignorance of things that I supposed I understood. Why, in the meeting at New York, on one occasion there was debate in which many men took part, and it was found that the meeting was almost evenly divided, although there was a decided majority on a point that involved a question of only 5 per cent, and those who thought one way convinced those who thought the other way, so that when the debate was over they were all of one mind.

That was a significant fact. But I observe this: that it was not thought to be an important matter. And yet, gentlemen, what is 5 per cent today? Measured by the experience of this successful organization, it is practically the measure of profit on the earned premium. And 5 per cent became a very important figure. What would have been the result if this debate had not taken place? What would be the result if the profit of that debate were not availed of by all of us? This—that in ignorance of the fact which involves the entire profit of the business, I might be cutting the rate of my friend the president of the Ætna, just as I am doing today, undoubtedly — in ignorance, not in greed—whereas, if I knew what he knows, I should let his risk severely alone and let him enjoy the profit of it. That is a significant fact, a very significant fact, that today the companies of this country, in ignorance, not in greed, are cutting each other's rates. But does that avail the president of the Ætna? I say no; he does not get the advantage of what he knows himself; for there are four thousand presidents of the Ætna company — resident presidents in Podunk, Oshkosh, Alton, Ill., Savannah — more potential than Mr. Clark in making the rates of the Ætna Insurance Company. Another very significant fact. And so that schedule must be educational, for it has brought out the opinions of men and secured the concurrent judgment of the underwriting ability of the country.

Now, what is the process of making a rate today? There are experts in this business, and a number of them—plenty in this room—men of judgment, men who are able to fill any position in the business, who inspect a risk carefully and express an opinion that you and I would bank upon. The merchant complains, "Your rate is too high; you charge me 60 cents on my building, and 1 per cent on my stock. It is too high. Tell me how you arrive at it." The answer is: "I arrive at it by expert judgment; by the very judgment by which you tell one piece of cloth from another. You cannot tell me why this is worth $2 a yard or that is worth $3, but you know the difference, although you may not be able to put it in words. In my business I am supposed to know the difference. I have been in the business twenty-five years; I represent the Old Reliable Insurance Company and know all the statistics."

But what happens? Inspector Doesticks, of the family of Doesticks that we have always with us, representing the Asinine Insurance Company of Donkeyville, comes on the opposite side of the street, takes one look at the building, rushes across, greets the merchant with the statement: "I think your building is not worth over 40 cents and the stock 60 cents." And the merchant says, "Give me your hand; I believe you are right; this ancient and venerable man who has been twenty-five years in the business ought to be graduated out of it; he has gone to seed."

Now if the schedule is too much in detail, the test of the detail is this: Is there a single thing in that schedule which has a price fixed which ought not to be taken into account in fixing the rates? Is there a single thing there that improves the building? If so, it ought to be recognized in the price. I want to call your attention to one of the points in the schedule which seems to us a very important one. It is that in the bulk of exceptional features, they are provided for by deductions. I do not need to elaborate on this point to a body of men like those that are listening to me—that wherever a very high standard is used for rating, where every departure from that standard must be charged for, there will be omissions inevitably; and that is a very dangerous sort of schedule which weighs coal with the troy scale or the diamond carat scale of the jeweler. There is no need of that. That alone would be a sufficient reason for the merit of that schedule in treating that scale of merit by deductions. They will be overlooked by some careless men; they will not be overlooked by the careful. We will not be the loser. I claim for that schedule this: that by its penalties, by its pointing out faults, such faults as have been pointed out by men all ever the country, it must save a great deal of money in pointing out what fires can be prevented.

We have heard one of the ablest insurance commissioners in this country name the number of fires in Massachusetts which could have been prevented, and he names some 2,500, and he tells how large a proportion were preventable. I have been over, as all of you have, probably, the figures of my own company, and I have the figures and percentages of a much greater number of fires than burned in Massachusetts last year. And I find that taking the percentage of each cause of the preventable kind —largely carelessness, largely defective flues—there are some 33 per cent of that character, of which 16 per cent are defective flues. The fires from unknown causes are 35 per cent, and it is fair to assume that one-third of those were preventable causes, if 33 per cent of those that we know about were; and 23 per cent were exposure fires, and it is fair to assume that 33 per cent of those were due to carelessness; and so between 50 and 90 per cent, at least, are due to things that would be pointed out by this schedule.

The other day I walked with my wife in New York to the grocery where she does her marketing, and as we stepped in I noticed that the floor was covered with sawdust, and I remarked to her that that was dangerous. As the proprietor stepped up at that moment she, laughingly, said, "My husband says this saw-dust is dangerous that you have on the floor; he is in the insurance business." He said, "Oh, no, Mr. Moore; we use steam heat." Of course I explained to him about the broken bottle of olive oil and spontaneous combustion. And I made this remark: "The underwriters will charge you 25 cents additional on $100, the first thing you know, and you had better use sand." That is all I said, but the next morning I passed there and there was no sawdust on the floor.

So, twenty-five years ago the proprietor of an establishment in Philadelphia told me why he had his barrels of sawdust on the sidewalk—that he had two fires break out in those in one day and so he had put them outside. One of our special agents said to

me the other day, " Coming upstairs the other morning I threw
away, as I had for years, a cigar stump, and it occurred to me
after I got into my office that I had thrown it into some place
where it might be dangerous, and I went back to see what I had
thrown it into. It was a sawdust spittoon." That is another important matter, and merely having a penalty attached to it will
have no effect. So I think you will agree with me that a system
of rating that will take all those faults and charge for them will
be all important.

A great deal has been said in our business about its not being
the duty of an underwriter to attempt to prevent fires, to have
anything to do with construction or fire department; that it is
our province to take risks as we find them and charge for them.
Now I do not believe that doctrine is entertained here. It does
violence to any supposition of the brotherhood of man, of the responsibility of each man to his fellow, and it lays an axe at the
very root and foundation of society. Every man, in some sense,
you know and concede without argument, is the brother of his
neighbor, and every man in his particular calling owes it to the
general community of which he forms a part to aid that community with the peculiar knowledge which he gains in his particular business. The underwriter ought to know more than the
chemist about fires and the cause of them; and if you read any
treatise on chemistry today you will find that the chemist glides
over those matters of spontaneous combustion and the origin of
fires with the same nonchalance and perhaps not so much
emphasis as on some chemical reaction that simply casts a white
precipitate. The underwriter ought to know more about building a flue or wall than any mason that ever handled a trowel.
He ought to know more about building around fireplaces or cutting the timbers away from chimneys than any carpenter that
ever handled a saw. He ought to know more about it than an
architect; the architect is simply occupied with looking out for
the beautiful, while the underwriter's knowledge and experience
go to the practical details affecting safety. He ought to know more
about electricity than Edison. He ought to know more about the

extinguishment of fires than a fireman, for his is the experience of a thousand cities instead of one. It is that particular knowledge that he gains that makes him debtor to his fellows. He ought to conduct his business in such a way that he shall encourage the safer construction of buildings; he will point out particular dangers that he has observed; he will have his eye upon fire departments; he will be doing his duty to the community in which he lives and will be contributing to the very safety of the country itself. He will be cutting down this enormous fire waste. The man who neglects that duty is certainly a traitor to the republic in which he lives. There is no escape from it. It is the duty of every man, it seems to me, to so conduct his business with such care, intelligence, and economical methods that he shall place his commodity to his consumer at the lowest possible price consistent with a fair and decent profit for himself.

Mr. President and gentlemen, I have heard tonight one saying that will ring in my ears for many a day. It was a striking illustration of the admonition of the toastmaster, "Brevity is the soul of wit." It seemed to me to touch the keynote of our duty as underwriters. It seemed to me so appropriate that this New England Insurance Exchange might well adopt it as its motto, that blazoned on its helmet, so to speak, it would win for it the appreciation of the public which we are seeking, and it seemed to me fitting. It was the utterance in the first speech of the evening by the first president of the New England Exchange, when he said—and I would like to see it on the walls of your meeting room—"We best serve the interests of our companies when we serve the interests of the public."

Mr. Sherman—"The Boston Board of Fire Underwriters." Our twin sister, born under the same influences as ourselves, may the ties of birth promoted by common interests and mutual confidence ever grow stronger. We will introduce a gentleman well and favorably known to the insurance men of Boston, one who for twenty consecutive years has been secretary of the Boston Board of Fire Underwriters, or similar organizations immediately preceding, Mr. Osborne Howes, Jr.

REMARKS OF OSBORNE HOWES, JR.

Mr. President, Mr. Toastmaster, and Gentlemen: I have a peculiar pleasure in being here tonight which I fancy only a few of the older members of the Exchange are aware of. I have sometimes wondered that in the official list of the past officers of the association my services for some time, for some months, as a species of secretary of the Exchange, were omitted. But I find tonight from the toast which has been read that I was hardly considered in the light of a secretary, but rather in the light of the useful and necessary, but not always honorable person of a midwife. I may be said to have acted in that capacity and to have helped Messrs. Crosby and Turner, Gray and Field, and others through the pains of parturition, and in nursing and swathing, and washing the young bantling until it had attained the age of two or three or four months, as the case may be, and when it got strong enough to get a boot and shoe factory schedule under way, and then turn it over to the tender mercies of my successor, James Bruerton.

But I am not here tonight to dwell upon reminiscences particularly, nor in following the example of my friend, Mr. Field, to dwell too much on the work of the Boston Board of Fire Underwriters except in an incidental way. I have but a very few minutes, because it is very late and there are other speakers, and the time is short anyway to expound what I have to say, and it is in a certain way a heresy, perhaps; at least it conflicts entirely with the general ideas of the gentleman who has just preceded me. I bring this point out for the reason that the universal schedule which he proposes to have generally adopted runs in conflict with the general theories of written risks which have by degrees been built up in Boston.

I think we all will concede that it is desirable and in the future will be necessary to form what may be termed a scientific system of underwriting. Now I think you will all agree with me that the nearest approximation to a scientific system has been attained by the life insurance companies; that they have a scale of certain charges modified very little from time to time, and it seems to me that the reasons that they have attained that end and have pursued for so many years their course successfully has been that they have held to certain broad, simple principles, and have not attempted to deal so much in questions of detail.

Now, if you will permit me, I should like to apply the general principles of detailed rating to a life insurance policy. We will assume first an ideal man, a perfect man, whose life will perhaps be one hundred years. We will also assume that he lives in an ideal community, where the rate of mortality is ten in a thousand. Now this man is the basis upon which all other lives are to be graded. The expectancy or non-expectancy of all other lives is to be determined by the life of this ideal man. An applicant goes into the office of a company, either in Boston or in New York, and the first question to him is where he lives. Well, he lives either in New York or Boston. The annual rate of mortality in one or the other of those cities is usually from twenty-two to twenty-five in a thousand; therefore we will add on that account $30 to the rate, making — we will assume the ideal man to pay $100, and we add $30, making $130, which would be the key rate by which the life was to be determined.

Now, the medical examiner goes through him as he does through most persons that apply and finds that his heart is somewhat weak—he has a tobacco heart. He adds $2.50 for that. Then his maternal grandmother died of pulmonary consumption; he adds $4 for that. His urine is not up to the specific gravity, and $4 is added for that. Then his father lived until he was 80 years of age, and $5 is deducted for that. I won't go through the long schedule; all of you know how the doctor goes through the individual characteristics of the man. And I say that it is possible for a life insurance examiner or a life insurance actuary to apply those various charges which would distinguish one man from the other, and in that way he would make out what would be an ideally perfect schedule, so that each man would be rated according to his merits. and the strong man would get the benefit of the low rate, and the weak man would have to pay an additional sum. As a matter of fact, while that would be ideal, the scientific system of life insurance would evaporate. It would be utterly impossible for actuaries of life insurance companies to lay down those general broad principles of action that they hold to at the present time, simply because you would have gone from a dealing in general averages down to a dealing in particulars, and where particulars vary so greatly it would be almost impossible to formulate any scheme of writing that would hold for any length of time.

Now to apply that to fire insurance — and now I bring it down to possibly a local application—we have found it as the result of our experience in Boston, so far as mercantile risks are concerned, or risks that are of a light manufacturing character, that we can serve the public best, we can content the public best, if we will put on what is practically the same rate for the same class of business. Assuming that the people occupy buildings that are fairly alike, the conditions of which cannot be changed except by a radical change — that is, tearing down or burning down the building and reconstructing it — we attempt in the boot and shoe industry, for example, to rate all classes about alike. Then in addition to that we have our system of inspection which goes through these various risks, and where it is found that there are correctible defects, those defects are charged for, and the charge remains upon them until corrected.

The effect of that has been in Boston very much more advantageous than when, a number of years ago, we attempted to apply a system of schedule rating to mercantile risks, bringing about very material differences, which could not be explained in a convincing manner to the occupants and owners of buildings. The result is that for years past we have had not the least friction with our public. I think that I may safely say that there is no city in the United States that for the last five years or ten years or twenty years can show a better rate of earning for the companies than Boston; that is, that the average of our fire losses, the percentage of fire losses to premium receipts, is as low here, if not lower, than in any large city in the United States, and has been so. And yet at the same time we have carried our public along with us, so that while they are willing to stand an advance of 20 per cent, as we have recently made it, or in individual cases, where we can point out to them correctible defects, they are willing to stand it. I do believe that if we were to change our system and to make these differences between men in the same trade, the effect would be disastrous to our organization, and we should have what we have not had during the last three or four years — attempts at breaking up all board organizations brought into the legislature.

Now I will go one step further and say that it is the duty, as Mr. Moore has said, of the underwriters to improve in every way they can the construction of buildings, so as to prevent the great fire waste which is annually taking place. It seems to me that in that respect the course we have adopted in Boston is the right one to take. Last year I had the pleasure of presenting to the legislature of this state the draft of a building law drawn up very carefully and which I think is a model in its way. If it is not a model I can only say that I am responsible for it, because I could have made it different if I had wished to. The only change the committee of the legislature made in that building law was to strike out the item that I had introduced prohibiting the use of wooden signs upon buildings. They objected to that and it was taken out, but with that exception the bill passed precisely as it was introduced, and it will apply, of course, to all new construction. But that is all that we can hope to do in a radical manner. No matter if we increase the rate upon a mercantile building two, three, or four times larger than it is, the owner of that building is not going to destroy that building and put up another. In time it will be taken down and a better one erected. But upon the principle of allowing the public authorities—just as the life insurance companies look to the boards of health to procure good sanitation, etc.—following that system, it seems to me the underwriters can do more good than by any attempt on their part to correct defects simply by a system of additional charges.

I thank you, gentlemen, for the attention you have given me. I am very glad indeed to have been here this evening, and while I have not expressed myself, perhaps, as plainly on this subject as I wish I could, I thought it desirable to take this occasion to do so.

Mr. Sherman—"Finance and Insurance." The interests of insurance and finance are so intimately interwoven that a cessation to furnish our policies of indemnity would paralyze the business community. We will introduce one of our New England financiers, a president of a leading New Hampshire bank, treasurer of a successful New England fire insurance company, a gentleman whose eloquent voice has been heard in the legislative halls of his state in friendly defence of insurance companies, Hon. G. B. Chandler of Manchester, N. H.

REMARKS OF G. B. CHANDLER.

Mr. Toastmaster and Gentlemen: I arise to express to you the great pleasure I have had in meeting with you this evening. Such gatherings as this must certainly be of great benefit. From the words of wisdom, the words of counsel, the kindly words which have been expressed here, you must certainly reap a rich harvest in the future. I was glad to hear Boston extolled by one of the leading underwriters in this city. While he was speaking the pride of my own state was kindled when I thought that he himself was a New Hampshire boy, when I thought that the president of this Exchange was a New Hampshire boy, when I thought that the secretary of this Exchange was a New Hampshire boy, when I thought that the first president of this Exchange was a New Hampshire boy; and when I looked about this board and saw seated here other sons of the Granite State who are largely interested in the insurance business of New England, I said, "New Hampshire certainly is at home; New

Hampshire has friends in this Exchange; we have friends at court." And when some one came along and whispered to me, "There are more special agents on this floor from New Hampshire than any other state," I said, "I will repeat that statement without vouching for it, for I cannot believe it to be true." Now, gentlemen, the hour is late, and I will take but a moment of your time. The subject assigned me is "Finance and Insurance." I presume I was invited to speak upon finance from the fact that I have had in one bank in New Hampshire an experience of thirty-eight years. That certainly should entitle me to be considered in the line of the financiers. Now what we do in the way of finance is to promote the business interests of the country as no other department of business can promote it. The work which is done by the financier or by the bank is a work which is surprisingly large. I suppose, as a matter of fact, that the exchanges as made through the clearing houses of this country are in the neighborhood of $200,000,000 a day. This is the work of the financier. He is adjusting balances, or rather, he is the medium through which balances are adjusted between individuals, between communities, between countries.

Now the value of the functions of the financier I wish I had the time to dilate upon, but I have not. The next interest that I would consider would be the insurance interest. Perhaps I was asked to consider that from this standpoint for the reason that for twenty-three years—the life of the New Hampshire Fire Insurance Company—I have been its treasurer. The record is one of which, from the financial standpoint, I feel, with the other members of our committee, very proud. Now what are we doing? What dependence have we—what reliance do we, as insurance people—place upon finance? Here is in this country an estimated wealth of between sixty and seventy billions of dollars. Of that amount more than twenty billions of dollars is covered by policies in companies which are represented by these gentlemen gathered around this board. More than twenty billions of property is protected by you. Now what should we as financiers do without the protection which we as insurance people give to this community? Where would be the credit of the merchant, where would be the credit of any class of people engaged in the enterprises of this country if their risks could not be insured and covered as you cover them with your insurance policies? Does this ever occur to you? Have you ever thought of the great responsibility which rests upon you having in charge this enormous interest?

Now, I am a little in the position of the young man who had two sweethearts, and they happened both to meet him together one day, and his ejaculation was, "How happy could I be with either, were t'other dear charmer away." I am so infatuated with both of these departments of business—finance and insurance—that I can do them no justice in a speech of five minutes, and consequently I shall do best not to try. I wish, however, to say before taking my seat that I agree very fully with the sentiment which has been uttered here tonight with regard to the protection of property. Mr. Moore told us of the cigar stump thrown into the sawdust spittoon and of seeing in a store the floor covered with sawdust. I once, in going through the establishment of the Armour Packing Company in Chicago with a Boston insurance man—the president of a Boston company—actually found the lighted stump of a cigar in the sawdust which covered the floor. I said to the president, "Now you and I had better get out of this business if that is the kind of risks we are taking here—cigar stumps thrown among the sawdust." It seems to me that it is the next thing to a crime that we should so allow the construction of buildings that the fire losses in this country can reach the enormous proportions of $130,000,000 to $140,000,000 a year. Gentlemen, make a study of this point. You, as insurance people, should take hold of it; you should endeavor to procure such legislation as should absolutely prohibit the erection of such buildings as now form a very large percentage of those which are being erected in the cities and villages in this country. Gentlemen, I thank you for your attention. The hour is late and I bid you good night.

Mr. Sherman—"Absent Friends, our Shareholders." Some one has well said, "Absence makes the heart grow fonder," and in proposing this sentiment we call to mind a suggestive stanza:

> "Count not the hours while their silent wings
> Thus waft them in fairy flight,
> For friendship warm from her deepest springs
> Shall hallow this scene tonight.
> And while the music of joy is here
> And the colors of life are gay,
> Let us think of those that we would were near,
> The friends who are far away."

We take much pleasure in introducing to respond to this sentiment the United States manager of the Norwich Union Fire Office, Mr. J. Montgomery Hare.

REMARKS OF J. MONTGOMERY HARE.

Mr. President and Members of the New England Exchange: I wish in coming to this banquet to lay before this assemblage my tribute of respect and admiration. The Exchange has since its organization ten years since, from its wise action and tendency to cultivate fraternal feeling among the field men, been a leader among all associations. Our occupation calls from those who occupy it a high grade of qualification. It is a profession which, if the highest standard is sought for by us will require more general information than most others. We must have knowledge of physics, of commercial customs, of law as laid down for us by legislature, of law as laid down for us by courts, and above all, a thorough knowledge of human character. It is but natural, therefore, that in New England and especially here in Boston that we should find so successful an organization as your Exchange. Much has been done by you, but much remains to be done. Through some condition—time tonight will not permit any attempt to explain why—we find the insurance business through extraordinary bad results in the last two years in a condition which requires some radical change.

An examination of statistics will show that the percentage of total loss to total amount insured remains about the same, but they also show that the average rate of premium to the amount insured has been reduced. Not on all kinds of business. There is a class we all know is carrying another class because of that class being written at inadequate rates. Now we have a condition that confronts us, that, in justice to "Absent Friends, our Shareholders," must be met. These friends have been very patient but they now call upon us for action. Absent friends are sometimes forgotten but at this time of congratulation and festivity let us have them in memory and around this board let the sentiment of the occasion fill us with the determination to join hands and bring about a proper recognition of their rights. We are by our failure to act undermining that strength of our corporations which is relied upon by the merchant and manufacturer to aid them in time of conflagrations.

A stock company must do more than pay losses and pay dividends; they must be allowed to set aside a fund such as will permit them successfully to meet such disasters as Boston and Chicago. As it is now we are but collecting and disbursing agencies—not always able to collect and not always able to disburse. The insuring public is not satisfied with this; it is prepared to pay us reasonable insurance rates at the present time to secure responsibility in time of great disaster. I will not enter upon how this should be done, you are competent to decide this, but if it is to be done let it be done at once.

And now before closing, Mr. President, there are other absent friends which we must have in remembrance and they are also shareholders, present and prospective—our wives and sweethearts—to the first we owe much in the encouragement given, to the latter much in the ambition stirred up. I ask you all to join in the toast, "Fair Women, Our Wives and Sweethearts."

Mr. Sherman—"The Fire Laddies," important allies to the insurance companies. Great interests depend on their ability, celerity, courage and persistence. The faithful fire men deserve the earnest sympathy and encouragement of insurance companies. We will introduce the fireman champion, the United States manager of the North British & Mercantile Insurance Company, Mr. Samuel P. Blagden.

REMARKS OF SAMUEL P. BLAGDEN.

Gentlemen: I would not allow you to wait another minute here, but for two reasons. The first is that of gratitude coming straight from the heart; and the second is, that the subject which was given to me relates to a department in which the public are properly more interested than ourselves, but with which we are so intimate that it is our pleasure and duty to speak a word in their behalf and of information to the public. My friend on my right and others have alluded to this city of Boston and to its growth, to its change. Let me in the beginning refer to it in another way. I am a native of this city. There exists in connection with it and its people one great peculiarity. No matter how long a native may be away, when he returns it seems like coming home. As I looked out of my window this morning I did not see a single thing with which I had not been familiar over forty years ago. In front of me was the Common and the old Frog Pond, covered with a mantle of purity. It was a morning such as that of which Lowell sang, when

> Every pine and fir and hemlock
> Wore ermine too dear for an earl,
> And the poorest twig on the elm-tree
> Was ridged inch deep with pearl.

If I had wanted anything else to make me feel that I was indeed at home, it is that unvarying cordial, nay, affectionate greeting, which I always receive from those who knew me in the years that are gone, emphasized as it is tonight in the cordial greeting which I receive from you. I remember walking, a beautiful summer's day, along this avenue, with her who is nearest and to whom I owe most, and as she looked at this city she said, "It is a beautiful city, and I love the people, but I do wish they wouldn't think so much of themselves." "Well," I said, "what can you expect, when people like you think so much more of them than they do of themselves."

But we may carry that thing too far, gentlemen. We have all become accustomed to hear and probably agree that anyone who was born in Boston doesn't need to be born again. But I must confess my amazement at the audacity which I have noticed displayed in the public prints by anyone asserting that Boston doesn't need any co-insurance clause. We all need that. It is the foundation stone of the system upon which we can arrive at the true proportion of losses, and thus at equitable rates.

Next to that, gentlemen, and with it, we need and cannot too much enforce upon every insurance department of this country the necessity for far more rigid building laws than exist in any portion of it today. The height and the area of buildings make them hazardous, as you know, for conflagrations, and not only that, but—in rushing hastily to the subject you have named for me—it makes it outrageously hazardous for our fire laddies. Now, if there is a city in the Union which should be thankful to the firemen, it is Boston. Go back with me, as some of you can, a score of years and a little more, and stand on the corner of old Milk street after acres of our city had been burnt over and millions of value consumed; stand there and hear those citizens, as they did, say to the fire laddies, "God bless you! Save the old church!" Those poor men, worn out, almost exhausted, put forth fresh energy at the call. They did save the old church and every cent of the church's property, and in so doing, mind you, they saved vastly more, for if that church had gone no human power could have stayed that fire from crossing Washington street and burning over acres and acres of territory.

You owe a great deal to the fire laddies. They are ever forgetful of themselves. Think of them in the coldest night, braving the blizzard and the tempest, as they were compelled to in New York. It is only a few weeks since I stood on top of one of the largest warehouses in Brooklyn and saw the bodies of two of those faithful fellows brought out of the ruins, standing as they had been on the merchandise, fighting the fire until it went in, and they went with those heavy bales and were lost. It is only two days since you all read in the papers of their persistent bravery in rescuing six men in that building where explosion followed explosion, never retreating in spite of the increasing danger, until they brought out every one of them, one to die, and the rest saved, though maimed. No, we cannot say too much for them.

I cannot close this without referring to an instance among our own more immediate fire laddies. Several of you have heard of it, but you will bear with me if I tell of it again, that we may honor ourselves in doing justice to the heroism of one of our own men. You will remember, for it was only a few months since, on that beautiful summer morning, when that awful catastrophe occurred, of the burning of the Hotel Royal in New York. The scene was a fearful one. The bodies of the dead and maimed victims were lying in the street. Men and women were jumping from the windows to almost certain death upon the pavements below, or falling back to perish in that sea of fire. The poor crowd in their interest were unable to withdraw their gaze from the scene, every incident of which was made only too distinct in the lurid glare of the flames. At a window in one of the upper stories was gathered a group of four. Among them was that sacred trinity, that God-given trinity of father, mother, and child, awaiting death together. At a window in the adjoining building appeared a sergeant of our patrol; he was unable to reach them. Without hesitation he threw himself down, locking his legs around a wire conveniently near, and holding himself upon the sill with his one arm, with the other he guided that group of four over his prostrate body as a bridge to that window and to safety.

His work was not yet through. Ascending to the roof in another portion of the building, he discovered a man standing upon one of the upper windows. Crying to him to wait and he would save him, he rushed to the street and calling upon two companions to follow him, ran to the roof of another adjoining building. He threw himself head first over the cornice, his companions holding him by the legs, and succeeded in getting that man of over two hundred pounds upon the roof. To that man I had the honor of presenting one of our medals, which is only given in the case of the saving of life. Gentlemen, in closing let me give you with all heartiness a toast you will gladly drink: " Our fire laddies, God bless them."

Mr. Emerson—*Gentlemen*: Before we sing our closing hymn I wish to announce that tomorrow—or perhaps I should say today —at 10 o'clock, the annual meeting of the New England Insurance Exchange will be held in its rooms at No. 55 Kilby street, and we should be glad to see you all there. I hope we shall have that pleasure. Now, if you will join me in singing " Auld Lang Syne," we will close our exercises for the night.

REGRETS FROM VARIOUS SOURCES.

From the letters received from prominent underwriters who were unable to be present at the banquet the following extracts are taken:

PHILADELPHIA, Pa., Dec. 5, 1892.

Please present our congratulations to the Exchange, and assure them of our continued fidelity and loyalty. The Exchange has been one of the most useful of all the tariff organizations; has been of incalculable value to the companies, and is deserving of the highest praise as well as the continued confidence and support of all the companies which it represents.

Yours very truly,

E. C. IRVIN, President,
Fire Association of Philadelphia.

HARTFORD, Dec. 27, 1892.

I am honored by your invitation to attend the reception and banquet given by the New England Insurance Exchange on the 6th of January next, and beg leave to express my profound regret that my office duties and other engagements prevent my acceptance and attendance. It is a gratification, however, for me to know that other gentlemen of our executive staff will share your hospitality on that pleasant occasion. The fact that the festive suggestion emanates from the New England Insur-

ance Exchange fully insures its success and an enjoyable
evening. Yours sincerely,
A. C. BAYNE, Vice-President,
Ætna Insurance Company.

NEW YORK, Dec. 27, 1892.

I have uniformly felt that the work of the Exchange has
been conducted with rare discretion and consistency. Deserving
as it does the highest commendation and support by the companies whose interests have been so successfully served, I trust
and believe the association will continue to exercise its good
judgment to the end that it may celebrate many happy returns
of the decennial dinner. Very truly yours,
HENRY W. EATON, Manager,
Liverpool & London & Globe.

CHICAGO, Ill., Dec. 16, 1892.

In giving expression to my regret that the exigencies of business will prevent me from being with you, let me add the assurance of hearty respect for the splendid organization that you
represent, and convey through you to your fellow-members in
behalf of the "Union" the kindest of greetings and the best of
good wishes. Very sincerely yours,
THOMAS J. CHARD, President,
"The Union."

MANCHESTER, N. H., Dec. 27, 1892.

Trusting that those assembled will have all the enjoyment that
the intelligent and hard working members of this association
deserve, and that when all is over and inspiring sleep has
refreshed the body and cleared the head, they will each buckle
on their armor with renewed energy and go for the risks that
won't burn. With a high appreciation of the character of the
members individually, and of their services in behalf of the
insurance interests of New England collectively, and with sincere thanks for the honor of the invitation,
I remain, yours very truly,
JAMES A. WESTON, President,
New Hampshire Fire Insurance Company.

STATE HOUSE, BOSTON, Dec. 19, 1892.

I thank your Exchange for its very kind invitation to attend its
reception and banquet on the evening of Jan. 6. I regret very
much to say that I have an important engagement for that
evening which makes it impossible for me to be present at the
dinner. There is, however, a chance that I may be able to be
with you for a little while at your reception. I certainly hope
I may have this pleasure, as I would like extremely to meet the

members of your Exchange and their invited guests. It is a great disappointment to me that I am not able to be with you through the evening, and to have the opportunity of expressing to the Exchange the interest of the Commonwealth in your work and her best wishes for your continued prosperity.

Very truly yours,

WILLIAM E. RUSSELL, Governor.

NEW YORK, Dec. 16, 1892.

It is with peculiar pleasure, in my travels throughout the United States, that I learn of the esteem and respect which the New England Exchange enjoys. Permit me to offer my congratulations and hearty good wishes for the continued success of an organization distinguished for its consistent and able management, its good influence, and good fellowship. Yours very truly,

WILLIAM A. FRANCIS, Assistant Manager,
North British & Mercantile Insurance Company.

CHICAGO, Ill., Dec. 29, 1892.

Being one of the early members of the Exchange, I have continued to follow eagerly all information I could secure of their doings from time to time, and am exceedingly proud of the record so far made and the very high esteem in which it is held by underwriters all over the world. That the commemorative exercises will be very interesting and enjoyable to the participants goes without saying and I am only sorry that I cannot arrange matters as to admit of my being present. Yours truly,

H. E. EDDY, Manager Western Department,
Commercial Union Assurance Company.

TORONTO, Dec. 21, 1892.

It requires great self-denial to say "no" to an invitation to meet the brightest and brainiest association of insurance men in the East, and I would gladly be a listener to the good things which will be said, and do full justice to your good cheer, if it were at all possible to do so, but I am just now expatriating myself and making an effort to set up my "lares and penates" in Toronto, and cannot possibly get a single day to devote to the duties of good-fellowship. Please to extend my thanks to your association for the honor of the invitation and accept my hearty good wishes for the success of your anniversary banquet and the prosperity and permanency of the New England Insurance Exchange.

A. A. CRANDALL,
Western Assurance Company.

Other gentlemen sending in their regrets were Messrs. Livingston Mims, W. F. Crook, E. E. Lowenguth, and C. W. Brownell.

CHRONOLOGICAL HISTORY OF THE EXCHANGE.

The New England Insurance Exchange was organized Jan. 6, 1883. Previous to its inception the fire insurance situation in this section can be best designated as chaotic. Rates, rules, and order were practically unknown at any point, and very few local boards were in existence. At Boston the local board had for some time attempted to control rates, which probably gave considerable moral support to the Exchange when organized.

The first attempt to make rates outside of Boston was in November, 1882, when a meeting of special agents was called to consider paper mills. It resulted in the sending out of a circular asking the companies if they would hold to rates on such risks if made. Forty-four companies answered that they would. Another meeting was held soon after and rates on lumber at Burlington, Vt., were made, which were promptly adopted by the companies.

The success attending these efforts led to an attempt soon after to rate jewelry factories at Attleboro, Mass., and at Providence, R. I. At a meeting of specials, held in the rooms of the Boston Fire Underwriters' Union, Dec. 11, 1882, a committee of five was appointed to perform the work. At the same meeting a committee was appointed to report on the use of naphtha in printing and lithograph establishments. A further step was taken in the adoption of a motion that it was the sense of the meeting that rates should be made for Lynn, Mass.

The spirit of organization had been in the air for some time, and at this meeting it was suggested that every Monday, at 11 A. M., the special agents meet "for the purpose of discussing subjects in which they are interested." The meeting adjourned before any action was taken; but at a meeting held a week later the subject was again brought up and discussed. As a result, the following was adopted:

Whereas, the weekly meetings of the New England special agents are believed to be of great interest to those in attendance, as well as of great value to the companies represented; therefore, resolved, that a committee of five be appointed by the chair to prepare some plan by which these informal meetings may be made permanent, and thereby secure a continuance of benefits now being derived.

A committee was appointed for the purpose. This committee, without delay, took the matter in hand and reported two weeks later recommending the organization of the " Exchange," with a personal membership open to field men only. No company was to be pledged to any action, reliance being placed on the honor of the specials to secure their co-operation.

The report was received with great favor and unanimously adopted. Thirty-six specials were present. Officers were elected, U. C. Crosby being made president.

Thus the " Exchange " was organized and launched upon its career. Its name was changed soon afterward to the " New England Insurance Exchange." In the meantime the committee on jewelry factories reported recommending a form of policy for these risks, which was afterward adopted by the companies, and a committee consisting of one special for each agency at Attleboro was appointed to make risks on factories in that place. It was deemed expedient to make no rates in Providence at that time.

A joint meeting of the Exchange and the local agents from Lynn, Mass., was secured, resulting in the formation of a local board in that place and the rating of brick and wooden shoe factories. A local board had also been formed at Springfield and a few rates established. Here some trouble was encountered, owing to the refusal of the agents to admit the Springfield F. & M., on the ground that its local representative was on a salary. The Exchange voted that the company should be admitted and gave the special Springfield committee full power to act.

The second meeting of the Exchange was held Jan. 13. The local committees already appointed and those to be appointed were then made standing. The executive committee reported a list of carefully-prepared by-laws, most of which are in vogue today. A committee was appointed to rate boot and shoe factories. This action involved the most extensive effort yet made in the line of rating. Rates for Worcester county, Mass., New Haven, and West Winsted, Conn., were also discussed.

The Exchange was now fairly under way and the development of its work was carried forward with increased enthusiasm. New members came in rapidly, committee work grew apace, and local boards were formed in various sections. So strong was the faith in the power of the new organization that as early as Jan. 27, 1883, it was suggested that a committee be appointed to defeat, by " legitimate means," proposed valued policy legislation in Maine. The suggestion was not adopted, however, and a resolution asking companies to withdraw if the law passed met with the same fate. The naphtha hazard, which had been discussed for a long time, was disposed of by making a charge for its use. A boot and shoe schedule was adopted and minimum rates placed on detached storehouses and contents. All this occurred within the first month of the organization.

The first year of Exchange work was necessarily experimental, but an immense amount of practical and permanent work was accomplished. The specials were found willing and active, and by the close of the year the larger portion of New England was in the hands of local committees and rated. During the year fifty-six local boards were formed and specific ratings made on paper mills, boot and shoe factories, straw shops, rubber works, summer hotels, fertilizer and chemical works, special hazards about Boston, tanneries and currying shops, cotton and woolen mills, and hat factories. The Exchange then numbered ninety-two members.

Evidence of the powers and facilities for good given by the organization was shown in several cases where the water supplies and fire department of various localities were deficient. This was most strongly shown in the case of Haverhill, where the persistent refusal to better the water supply resulted in an advance of forty cents in rates, which very soon brought the citizens of that place to their senses, and the desired reforms were secured.

The events of the succeeding years will be gone over briefly. President Crosby was re-elected for a second term, a distinction which he well deserved for the able manner in which he had served the Exchange during its first year. The work of this year was devoted largely to extending and perfecting the jurisdiction of the Exchange. More local committees were appointed, more local boards formed, and more rates made. Rates on boot and shoe factories were increased, and as a result this class of hazard was materially improved. Adequate classifications and ratings were also secured on cotton and woolen mills, paper mills, rubber works, tanneries, and summer hotels. Forty-three new tariffs were issued during the year and the number of local boards increased to 99, the standing committees to 129. Throughout the rating of the different classes and sections was carried on with diplomacy and system, very little friction being encountered. The committees performed their work in a spirit which won the confidence and support of local agents.

A matter which had long troubled stock underwriters in this section assumed a more serious aspect this year, viz: the competition of the factory mutual insurance companies, which were rapidly securing the cream of isolated and protected risks, which the stock companies were unable, apparently, to retain, largely because of ignorance regarding the insurance cost of this kind of risk. The subject was made one of considerable discussion in the closing annual address of President Crosby. He reviewed the situation carefully and pointed out that a systematic movement against the mutuals and an employment of their own weapons was the only salvation for the stock companies. This was the beginning of a movement which finally resulted in the present organized and successful system of competition employed in meeting the mutuals.

Mr. Crosby also drew attention to the necessity of co-insurance. He urged its adoption, and during the following year it was recommended by a special committee but failed to pass.

George P. Field, who was then in the front ranks of New England specials, succeeded Mr. Crosby as president. The task of rating had been practically completed and routine work was the settled order. The novelty of the situation having worn off and prosperity and harmony having been enjoyed for two years, trouble began to crop out in various localities. Mr. Field foresaw this, and in his inaugural cautioned great wisdom in the handling of questions of differences and the avoidance of hasty legislation. Although the year was a pivotal one and likely to have resulted in serious disruptions, extreme caution and fairness in considering all questions involving differences cemented the Exchange more strongly than ever, and made its position a sure and permanent one.

The most important event of the year was the withdrawal of the companies from New Hampshire following the enactment of the valued policy bill. In this move President Field proved beyond question his ability as a leader. He was well backed, however, by the members of the Exchange. The New Hampshire compact is famous throughout the country, and the rigidity with which it was adhered to through the five years of its existence is commonly looked upon as an evidence of the great ability manifested in this section to stand firmly and unitedly on an issue involving general principles.

At the close of this year the Exchange had extended its jurisdiction to all possible territory in New England. During the year special committees on "gasolene and kerosene heating and lighting" and "electric lights" were appointed, and both performed active work in supervising the hazard supposed to exist in this connection. Much was done toward improving the fire department and water supply facilities of various towns. Legislation on the division of commissions was passed and bore good results.

Mr. Field declined re-election for a second term, owing to his appointment as manager of the Royal, and George W. Taylor was unanimously elected his successor. Rates having now been firmly established, committee work consisted largely in re-inspecting and re-rating, owing to the great number of improvements made in risks under the healthy influence of established rates. Particular attention was given special hazards and the question of mutual competition. As a result, one of the most important moves since the organization of the Exchange took place, viz.: the appointment of the now well-known "factory improvement committee," whose duties were to investigate and pass upon automatic sprinklers and other protective devices, to have full charge of sprinkled risks and to make the rates thereon, and to confer with mill owners in order that mutual competition might be successfully met.

During Mr. Taylor's administration the Exchange, realizing the important part electricity was to assume as a factor in fire insurance, appointed an expert electrician to inspect all electric light plants in New England. The inspector soon gained the confidence and respect of the electric light companies, who welcomed the co-operation of the Exchange in the extension of safe installation.

In his closing address President Taylor pointed out the desirability of an insurance library, which had previously been suggested by Henry E. Hess, and the latter, as the successor of Mr. Taylor, brought this project into successful fruition. The outlining of the plan of this library was the main suggestion contained in the inaugural of Mr. Hess. During the year it was perfected through an immense amount of hard work on the part of those who labored to put it through. It was too plainly beneficial, however, to suffer materially from the obstacles in the way. The position it occupies today, the use to which it is put, and its undoubted permanency and financial stability amply repays for the efforts expended in placing it upon its feet.

During the administration of Mr. Hess an effort was made to secure united inspection by the Exchange, but the scheme failed of adoption, and was later carried out independent of the Exchange. The work of the new factory improvement committee progressed finely, and the effort to fairly meet mutual competition on its own grounds proved a success from the start. The question of co-insurance was again taken up, but nothing further was done than the granting of a reduction for the three-quarters

clause on buildings in one large city. Mr. Hess called attention
to the necessity of moving to larger quarters, owing to the
increase of Exchange work. He refused to be a candidate for
re-election, though strongly urged to accept.

Henry R. Turner was elected his successor. The permanency
of the Exchange was now secured beyond question, and Mr.
Turner aimed to improve and solidify the organization rather
than to branch out into any new fields. A significant event was
the removal of the Exchange quarters to the present location,
55 Kilby street. A five years' lease was secured, thus showing
the faith of the field men in the permanency of their association.
Rooms adjoining for the new library were also secured at the
same time. The competition of dwelling house mutuals was
a subject of discussion during the year, but no definite action
was taken. The results of the year proved eminently satisfactory and much was accomplished in its detailed work.

The next president, Benjamin R. Stillman, guided the Exchange with a careful hand and cemented more strongly the ties
which bound the special agents together. Although he again
called attention to the need of co-insurance, no action was taken
on the subject during that year. The occupancy of the new
quarters proved highly beneficial to the Exchange, in adding
facilities for performing its increasing work. On Mr. Stillman's
recommendation the constitution was amended to provide for
honorary membership, and he was one of the first to receive its
benefits.

During this year the New Hampshire compact was broken.
This compact was entirely a company affair but had received the
firm moral support of the Exchange, and the special agents
regretted, almost to a man, that it should be nullified. Some
who did not realize the full strength of the Exchange predicted
dissolution at this time. It stood firm as a rock, however.

Under President Frank A. Colley, who followed Mr. Stillman,
the Exchange enjoyed a quiet and prosperous year. The average attendance was the largest to date. The question of
dwelling house rates came to the front and the special committee

made an exhaustive report recommending a classification of these risks. After much discussion the matter was referred to the executive committee, and it has not since been considered. A pleasant diversion from routine work was the appointment of a committee to collect funds for the families of the firemen killed in the Boston conflagration of November. As a result, $1,200 was secured for the purpose. The Electric Mutual was formed this year by S. E. Barton, and competition on electric risks became quite lively. Through the efforts of President Colley the rule refusing information to the insurance press was rescinded.

In the election of officers for 1891 an unusual, though entirely pleasant, complication occurred in the selection of president. Moses R. Emerson was first nominated, but positively declined. A. C. Adams then became the popular candidate, and in spite of his earnest protest was elected. He presented his resignation at the next meeting and, as he gave good and sufficient reasons, it was accepted. U. C. Crosby was then elected and entered upon his third term.

Eor several years the Exchange had been sailing in smooth water, but conditions were changing, and it was evident that serious consideration must soon be given to such important questions as co-insurance, commissions, and a revision of rates. Moreover, bad practices were cropping out in some places, and the paying of high commissions had become a standing evil. The increased fire waste also called for action on the question of rates, and during Mr. Crosby's administration the conviction that an advance was necessary grew in common with a similar conviction throughout the country. It was a preparation for the large amount of legislation which followed under President Moses R. Emerson, who was elected to succeed Mr. Crosby. This brief chronological record of the Exchange will be closed with a rapid review of the legislation of 1892.

The drift in the direction of higher rates assumed definite form in December, 1891, when a proposition was introduced to advance rates 25 per cent, or require a 75 per cent co-insurance clause. The proposition was referred to a special committee, which reported favoring the 25 per cent advance but making the 90 per cent co-insurance clause the alternative. The matter was not discussed by the Exchange until the first meeting in January, but in the meantime a committee meeting of the whole was held and the question thoroughly talked over. It was supposed from this that an agreement would be easily reached when the matter was taken up in open meeting. It turned out, however, that there was much difference of opinion and no action was taken until a special meeting held the next week, when by general consent the co-insurance question was ruled out and a committee of nine appointed to recommend advances in rates in such places and on such classes as it was deemed advisable, this course being preferable to a general advance.

This committee carried out its work expeditiously but not with undue haste. An advance in Lynn, Mass., was almost immediately recommended and adopted. The committee also recommended an advance of 50 per cent on clothing stocks and factories, and a reduction therefrom of 25 per cent if a clause was contained in the policy stipulating that no claim should be made for smoke damage. The committee thereafter recommended advances in Vermont, and in Brockton, Springfield, Marlboro, Revere, and Winthrop, Mass.; also on large area risks; also on unprotected property and farm property in Maine. Revised schedules for boot and shoe factories and morocco factories were also put through.

In securing the adoption of these advances by local boards considerable opposition was encountered, particularly on account of the clothing advance and that made on unprotected property. So determined and persistent was this opposition — though many of the objecting boards were persuaded to come into line —that after over six months' delay the Exchange voted to put the rates arbitrarily into force, giving local committees discretion to waive the enforcement of advances if deemed expedient. This stand has given rise to some discussion and difference of opinion, but the majority seem to be in favor of exercising the arbitrary power to which they claim the Exchange is entitled.

The Exchange has always held that it had no right to interfere with the companies on the question of commissions, therefore this matter did not receive the attention it merited, but a 15 per cent compact was formed by the companies independent of the Exchange, though the latter afterwards adopted a 10 per cent brokerage rule and by timely action assisted the Boston board in clinching the question of brokerages.

In the latter part of the year the Exchange followed the Boston board in the adoption of the 80 per cent co-insurance clause. The action on this question is too fresh in mind to require detailed reference. It was adopted largely because the companies demanded it and were asking local organizations all over the country to adopt it. In New England the clause is mandatory on all specifically rated risks under Exchange jurisdiction, with the exception of risks rated by the factory improvement committee and the paper, pulp, and leather-board committee.

These are the more important matters of legislation during 1892, though many other significant changes were made, particularly in remodelling the rules of the Exchange. Altogether the year proved probably the most eventful one since organization, and despite the many obstacles encountered it has emerged better equipped for successful work in the future, and with a larger realization of the duties incumbent upon the special agent and the organization of which he is a member.

THE PRESIDENTS OF THE EXCHANGE.

Collectively the presidents of the New England Insurance Exchange represent the best field men that have been produced in this section, and though individually the common traits of character may be few, each has been peculiarly qualified to assume the position of leadership. The Exchange presidency has always been regarded as a post of great responsibility, and care in selection invariably characterizes elections for this office. Strong men are needed and strong men have been secured in every case.

U. C. Crosby was the first president of the Exchange, coming into that office as a natural result of his activity in bringing about its organization. He is a man of few words but many ideas, and probably takes a broader view of the scope of fire insurance than any underwriter in New England. He believes in meeting the assured more than half way, and the labor he has expended in developing protected business has contributed immeasurably toward recovering the ground lost by the stock companies to their competitors, the factory mutuals.

Mr. Crosby was born in Mattapoisett, Mass., in 1845, and was brought up at Bethlehem, N. H. In 1866 he entered the office of the Bay State Insurance Company of Worcester as clerk, and three years later was made secretary of the company, which office he held until the Boston fire of 1872, when the company suspended after paying 90 cents on a dollar. He then became special agent of the Commercial Union for New England. He remained with this company for eleven years, the last five of which he acted as its general agent. During this period he was also for a time secretary of the Shawmut Insurance Company of Boston. He then resigned to accept the special agency of the Phenix of Brooklyn for New England, which position he now holds.

He has been three times elected president of the Exchange, serving in 1883, 1884, and 1891. He is now chairman of the factory improvement committee, which he has thoroughly organized and brought up to a high standard of efficiency in competing for sprinkled business. Mr. Crosby has been interested particularly in developing the social side of the field man's life and has played the host on several memorable and successful occasions.

George P. Field succeeded Mr. Crosby in 1885. Mr. Field is generally described as the ablest and most popular underwriter in New England. His popularity is not of the kind that depends on a consideration, but has been fairly earned. His ability has placed him among the first underwriters in the land. Possessed of a keen intellect and a large fund of natural energy, his rise, since he came into prominence as a field man, has been rapid. He is decidedly a man of brilliant attainments, unusual intellectual capacity, and great personal magnetism.

Mr. Field was born at Searsmont, Me., Oct. 17, 1844. He acted as clerk in his father's agency at Belfast for several years. In 1866 he became assistant secretary of a local company at Bangor and later moved to Worcester and became secretary of the First National, the only Worcester company which survived the Boston fire. In 1873 he came to Boston as special agent of the Royal, under Foster & Scull. Here he was successively made general agent and superintendent of agencies, and finally a member of the firm in 1886. The firm at present is Scull & Field.

At the age of 20 he manifested remarkable executive ability, when he was appointed deputy provost marshal during the war and handled a clerical force of fifty to seventy-five men in drafting and enlisting about five thousand men a year. His duties then were arduous and required careful management, to which he proved amply equal. He was also deputy collector of customs for a time.

Having retired in his capacity as manager from field work during his presidency, he was not eligible for the re-election which would certainly have been his under other circumstances.

George W. Taylor, who was elected president in 1866, is a man of large abilities, wide experience, and innumerable possibilities, who has voluntarily sacrificed certain advancement in one direction to secure certain success in another. He began his field work in 1876, succeeding H. E. Bowers as special agent of the North British & Mercantile. Here he remained for twelve years, until he was appointed general agent for New England of the London & Lancashire. Jan. 1, 1891, he was advanced to the position of assistant manager for the United States of the London & Lancashire and removed to New York, where a most successful managerial career opened up for him. He resigned his position in October, 1891, however, to become a member of the firm of Blake & Taylor, one of the largest and most successful local agencies in Boston. As a local underwriter he is fast coming to the front, demonstrating that his abilities in this direction are equal to his capacities as a manager.

Henry E. Hess became president in 1887, having been but three years located in this field when his rare good judgment and firm, unswerving characteristics marked him as a man eminently fit for leadership. Mr. Hess is distinctly individual in his views, but thoroughly consistent and logical. He is a man of original ideas and quick perceptions and is one of the most competent adjusters in this section. He originated the plan of the Insurance Library and to his untiring zeal in the face of the most discouraging opposition is due its present permanence and success. He is also credited with having suggested a bureau of inspection as early as November, 1884, and was afterwards one of the most active in the organization of the New England Bureau of United Inspection.

Mr. Hess is now 41 years old. At the age of 16 he entered the fire and life office of Martin, Hopkins & Follett at Indianapolis, Ind., where he developed an aptitude for fire insurance. At 18 he went into a mercantile house at Portsmouth, O., but returned to Columbus, O., at the end of three years and entered his father's life insurance office. In 1876 he moved to Scranton, Pa., and engaged variously in the study of law, as editor of a daily newspaper, and as general insurance adjuster. He soon after became special agent of the Merchants' of Newark for the Eastern states, and was also two years with Charles R. Knowles of Albany, N. Y., as special agent of the Royal, Insurance Company of North America, and Pennsylvania. In 1884 he became New England special of the Connecticut Fire, the position he holds today.

Henry R. Turner, who became president in 1888, is a diplomat, a ready speaker, and one of the most successful general agents in this section. He has always been active in Exchange matters and has contributed a large share toward moulding its legislation. During the first year of the Exchange he was made chairman of the summer hotel committee and has retained the office ever since. Naturally he is the best posted man in New England on this class of risks.

Mr. Turner is a native of Norwich, Conn. His early insurance experience was with the Thames Insurance Company of Norwich, afterwards in New York with the Yonkers and New York Fire, and later with the Fairfield Fire Insurance Company of Connecticut, first as general agent and afterward as secretary. He experienced the great Chicago and Boston fires in the adjustment of losses and obtained here good groundwork for his future career. He entered the service of the Niagara in 1880 and for the past twelve years has been its general agent for New England excepting Connecticut. The general agency of the Caledonian of Scotland has been recently given him for this territory.

Mr. Turner was a prominent mover in the early organization of the Exchange and was secretary of the first meeting of field men called to rate paper mills. He was chairman of the executive committee in 1886.

Benjamin R. Stillman assumed the presidential chair in 1889. Being a man of pronounced views and decided opinions, which he always backs by plain statements and sound argument, he is universally liked and as president of the Exchange enjoyed widespread popularity.

Mr. Stillman was born at Adams, N. Y. He attended high school at Oswego, N. Y., and while there O. H. Hastings, president of the board of education and a member of the insurance firm of Mollison, Hastings & Dowdle, offered a position in his office to the boy standing highest in his examinations. Mr. Stillman secured the position and began his career as an insurance man. In 1872 he became a member of the firm of Shepard & Stillman. Soon after he was appointed special agent of the Watertown Fire, and was retained in a similar capacity by the Sun Fire when that company reinsured the Watertown. To him was assigned the difficult task of securing the admission of the Sun Fire to the Middle and Southern States without the home office statement of the company, which had always been required of foreign companies up to that time, a task which he performed with eminent success. In 1884 he was appointed to succeed the late W. T. Steere as general agent of the Springfield F. & M.

At the close of his presidential year Mr. Stillman left the insurance business, being induced by a flattering offer to engage in the gas business in New York City. One year was enough, however, to show him that the attachments and fascinations of insurance could not be broken off, and in February, 1891, he accepted an appointment as assistant secretary of the National of Hartford, where he is now located and working for good insurance with his old-time enthusiasm and ability.

Frank A. Colley, who was elected president in 1890, is one of the ablest, most active and successful managing special agents New England has produced. He is a man who talks little but does much and consequently has moved steadily upward in his insurance career. He was born in Newmarket, N. H., in 1852. In 1867 he began his business life with John Sise at Portsmouth, remaining there three years, when he entered the office of Foster & Cole of Boston, who, in addition to the local agency of several companies, had just been appointed New England general agents of the Franklin of Philadelphia. After doing a little incidental work here, such as copying letters, delivering policies, etc., and proving of little value in that capacity he was promoted to be assistant to the clerk of the Franklin agency department, and at the end of two months was made chief clerk, holding this position until **1880**, when he was appointed special agent of the Union of Philadelphia for New England. After building up a splendid business for this company he resigned, in 1889, to take the special agency of the New Hampshire. Two years later he was made general agent of the company, having charge of its entire agency business, and in the same year stepped into his present position as agency superintendent of the London & Lancashire in the New York office.

Mr. Colley was one of the original members of the Exchange and continually active in its work, being vice-president for two terms and a member of the executive committee for two terms. He was a member of the committee on whose recommendation the factory improvement committee was started.

Moses R. Emerson is the last in the line of presidents, and has just closed an administration in which more important legislation has occurred than in any previous year. Mr. Emerson is a man of liberal views who has aimed, by looking fairly on both sides of the shield, to reduce contention and differences to a minimum. He is wholly impartial, having given his best time and best thought toward steering the Exchange bark clear of the many rocks which have appeared in its course. As general agent of a leading and influential company he has sunk his personal interests to serve the highest interests of the Exchange, thus making an ideal presiding officer.

Mr. Emerson was born at Newport, N. H., and from 1853 to 1855 was engaged in mercantile pursuits at Ludlow, Vt. He then removed his business to Claremont, N. H., where in 1866 he established an agency, representing the Home, Hartford, Phœnix (Conn.), and Ætna. In 1873 he was made special agent of the Home for Maine, New Hampshire, and Vermont. He removed to Concord in 1887, remaining ten years, and then came to Boston, having been appointed New England general agent of the Home, which is his present position. Prior to his connection with the insurance businesss he was bank commissioner of New Hampshire for four years, and a member of the legislature for two years.

THE SECRETARIES OF THE EXCHANGE.

Osborne Howes, who was the first secretary of the Exchange, served in that capacity for a short time and was succeeded by James Bruerton, who also occupied that position but temporarily. The former is now secretary of the Boston board while the latter is district manager of the German American for Boston and one of the most respected underwriters in this city. He was succeeded as secretary by Arthur A. Clarke, who occupied the position for nearly five years, serving the Exchange faithfully and finally retiring on account of ill health. He is now acting as an independent adjuster. He was succeeded by Oliver P. Clarke, who resigned after two years' service to engage in the electrical business, but has since returned to the field of insurance under General Agent Emerson of the Home.

The present secretary, C. M. Goddard, was appointed to the position after having served for some time as electrical inspector of the Exchange. He was born at Claremont, N. H., in 1856, and graduated from the Chandler School of Science of Dartmouth College in 1877, when he became instructor of higher mathematics and natural sciences at the Episcopal Academy at Cheshire, Conn. In 1880 he became engaged in the banking business in New York, but in 1884 removed to Plainfield, N. J., and entered the electrical business, where he remained until appointed inspector of the Exchange. Here he rapidly grasped insurance ideas and since being appointed secretary has demonstrated great capacity, having thoroughly systematized the immense detail work of the Exchange. In addition, his practical knowledge as an electrician has proved of great value to the Exchange. He was a leader in the recent effort to perfect rules regarding electric installation.